TABLE GRACE

In our experience of pastoral leadership an open home is usually the sign of an open heart. Douglas Webster offers a thoughtful and biblical explanation of the value of hospitality and the importance of 'table grace'. The relevant questions that conclude each chapter help the reader understand why meals with meaning matter. We warmly commend this timely book.

Ian and Ruth Coffey
Moorlands College, Christchurch, Dorset

Doug Webster is a seasoned pastor and a remarkable teacher and preacher of God's Word. In this book, he weaves a biblical tapestry of hospitality, revealing its connection to worship, prayer and the renewal of the church today. A wonderful introduction to a major theme of Scripture. Readable, wise, and engaging.

Timothy and Denise George
Beeson Divinity School, Samford University, Birmingham, Alabama

TABLE GRACE

THE ROLE OF HOSPITALITY IN THE CHRISTIAN LIFE

DOUGLAS WEBSTER

CHRISTIAN
FOCUS

Doug Webster mentors future pastors at Beeson Divinity School in Birmingham, Alabama. He holds a Ph.D. from the University of St. Michael's College, Toronto School of Theology. He and his wife Virginia have served churches in New York, California, Colorado, Indiana and Canada. They have three adult children.

Copyright © Douglas D. Webster 2011

ISBN 978-1-84550-752-7

Published in 2011
by
Christian Focus Publications
Geanies House, Fearn, Ross-shire,
IV20 1TW, Scotland

www.christianfocus.com

Cover design by Moose77.com

Printed by Bell and Bain, Glasgow

CONTENTS

To Jean and Otis Froning
in gratitude for their hospitality

Foreword

Hospitality comes in many forms. When we first moved to Birmingham to teach at Beeson Divinity School, Virginia stayed behind in San Diego to sell our home. Brad and Wendy Allison didn't know me, but they heard from a friend that I needed a place to stay. They opened up their basement apartment to me free of charge and graciously provided a home away from home for seven months. Their love and generosity made the transition possible, and I am grateful for their hospitality.

Over the years, table fellowship with students, friends and family has been a forum for spiritual formation. Following the weekly chapel at Beeson, students and faculty meet for a community lunch subsidized by the school. I am sure the combination of worship and eating together is more valuable than we realize. For the last three years, our life in Birmingham has been richer because our daughter Kennerly and her husband Patrick lived with us as they completed their seminary education. At least twice a week we ate dinner together. We spent hours around the dinner table processing biblical studies, preaching, church life and pastoral theology. Eating and prayer go together. The table is the place where theology and ministry get worked into real life.

For the past year, Virginia and I have travelled to New York City every weekend to preach and pastor at Central Presbyterian Church. The church provided a one-bedroom apartment for our use, which made it possible to carry on this ministry. In New York we have enjoyed numerous meals with the church family. One of the elders, Jim Johnson, has the gift of hospitality. He has brought us together over dinner many times to enjoy fellowship and to discuss the church.

The Lord's hospitality extends from welcoming friends to skilled editors such as Jim Meals, Jason Fincher, and especially Rebecca Rine who have freely shared their gifts and made this a better book. The origins of this work go back to the faithful believers of First Presbyterian Church of San Diego who for fourteen years demonstrated a true receptivity to the Word of God. Their love for the Word and Christ encouraged me to be a better pastor and writer. In the end, the effectiveness of this book depends upon the hospitality of the reader. May God's grace open our minds and hearts to the beauty of his truth even if the writer, doesn't use enough seasoning.

1

The Invitation

Taste and see that the Lord is good.

Psalm 34:8

God's invitation to table fellowship can be found throughout the Bible. A simple meal is one of the best places to
begin to understand and practice true spirituality. Jesus invited more people to lunch than He did to the synagogue.
To the surprise of many, eating and prayer belong together.
Devotion to God and friendship with one another meet
'around the table,' so to speak. God designed us in such
a way that the measure of our communion with Him is reflected in the depth of our relationships with others. Physical nourishment and spiritual sustenance were meant to
go hand in hand. Table fellowship reminds us that there
is a remarkable symmetry between our communion with
God and our community with one another. Life's meaning
happens at God's invitation.

Conversation around a simple meal may mean more to
the Lord than all the hype we generate in busy churches.
The act of opening our homes and our lives to friends
and strangers holds real promise for spiritual growth. It

is amazing how lunch together can build us up in Christ. Table fellowship in Christ is one of the best ways to experience the communion of the saints. The Holy Spirit has assured us that there is a deep-level mystery involved in hospitality. We meet Christ in the midst of relating to others. 'Truly, I say to you, as you did it to one of the least of these my brothers and sisters, you did it me' (Matt. 25:40). 'Do not neglect to show hospitality to strangers, for thereby some have entertained angles unawares' (Heb. 13:2).

Hospitality has greater rewards than most of us imagine: 'Whoever receives you receives me, and whoever receives me receives him who sent me' (Matt. 10:40). The measure of our openness to others reveals our intimacy with the One who said, 'Come unto me.' Søren Kierkegaard understood this: 'Oh, where heart-room is, there house-room always is to be found. But where was there ever heart-room if not in His heart?'[1]

One of the best-kept secrets about hospitality is that those who offer it benefit more than those who receive it. When we open the front door of our homes to friends and strangers, set the table, put on a meal, and break bread together, we invite God's blessing. We think of hospitality as giving to others, but what if hospitality is the Lord's way of bringing people into our lives who will give to us: the foreign student who enlarges our world, the homeless person who deepens our compassion, the missionary who causes us to pray more earnestly, the single mom who increases our family, and the neighbor whose next-door-presence trains us in practical love? We may be like the reluctant widow at Zarephath, entertaining the prophet Elijah, or like the eager-hearted Lydia hosting the apostle

---

1   Søren Kierkegaard, *Training in Christianity* (Princeton: Princeton University Press, 1944), p. 13.

Paul. Whether we are reluctant or eager, we should under-stand that hospitality was meant to be an opportunity, not an imposition.

Most of us lead very private, busy lives and complain that we experience little community. We tend to be over-programed, protective of our time and families, and pas-sive when it comes to inviting people over for a meal. We have every intention of reaching out to others, but our hos-pitality falls victim to a host of excuses—we're too tired, our lives are too hectic, the house is messy, we don't know what to serve, and the list goes on.

Yet hospitality remains one of Christ's most basic provisions for community. I am surprised at how much happens over meals in the course of salvation history. The Lord accomplishes extraordinary work over ordinary meals. In this most basic of ways, materiality and spirituality converge. Abraham invites the Lord to lunch with a simple and sincere invitation. He offers them something to eat to strengthen them for their journey (Gen. 18:5). The Lord applied the principle of hospitality to the Passover meal with the command that if a household was too small for a whole lamb, they could share the lamb with their neighbors (Exod. 12:4). The Lord set up the Tabernacle with a small table overlaid with gold to symbolize fellowship between Himself and His people. On the table was the bread of the Presence (Exod. 25:30). Even in the wilderness, Yahweh furnished a table for His people (Ps. 78:19). Manna in the morning meant God's miraculous provision for the Israelites' material needs (Exod. 16:15). Daily bread and God's redemptive blessing coincide in a down-to-earth way.

Throughout the Old Testament, table fellowship was a way of reaching out and bringing reconciliation. David promised Saul's descendent Mephibosheth a seat at his table for as long as he lived (2 Sam. 9:7). Nehemiah made room at his table for visitors from the surrounding nations (Neh. 5:17). After Ezra 'opened the book' and read from the Word of God, Nehemiah encouraged the people to celebrate: 'Go home and prepare a feast, holiday food and drink; and share it with those who don't have anything: This day is holy to God. Don't feel bad. The joy of GOD is your strength!' (Neh. 8:10, MSG). Clearly, eating in the Old Testament became an occasion for God's grace to become evident in both physical and spiritual ways.

BIBLICAL HOSPITALITY

Table fellowship fits into the New Testament narrative so unobtrusively that we can almost miss it. A simple meal was the context for much of Jesus' interaction with his disciples. The Master intended spiritual growth to occur during mealtime fellowship. In His ministry, physical and spiritual nourishment ran together in the ordinary course of daily life. He fed the body and the soul. Jesus broke bread with the disciples before instituting the Lord's Supper. His high-priestly prayer, the longest prayer recorded in the Bible (John 17), was prayed around the table. After His resurrection, He fixed breakfast for Peter and the disciples and led Peter to reconciliation (John 21:15-19). Before His ascension, Jesus promised the Holy Spirit over dinner with the disciples. Luke described the setting this way: 'As they met and ate meals together, he told them ... ' (Acts 1:4, MSG). The ambience must not have been super-spiritual, no incense or prepared liturgy – just a simple meal. Jesus' way of relating to people rules out any method or manner that is either artificially contrived or self-consciously 'spiritual.'

Jesus is authentic, and He models the way He expects us to relate to one another. If we pay attention, the way Jesus made Himself known becomes just as meaningful to us as His revelation. Method and message work together. The prologue to the Gospel of John ends with these words: 'No one has ever seen God; the only God, who is at the Father's side, he has made him known' (John 1:18). God-incarnate made the invisible God real to us by inviting Himself into our lives, not in some ethereal other-worldly sense, but in a way that really works in our ordinary daily lives. In His humility, Jesus invites our hospitality: 'Behold, I stand at the door and knock. If anyone hears my voice and opens the door, I will come in to him and eat with him, and he with me' (Rev. 3:20). The experience of Jesus' table grace makes us one with Him in revealing the invisible God. Love reigns around the Lord's family table. I John 4:12 parallels John 1:18 and reads, 'No one has ever seen God; if we love one another, God abides in us and his love is perfected in us.' In the Gospel of John, Jesus is the revelation of the invisible God. In the Epistle of John, those who love one another reveal the invisible God. Table grace transforms our lives.

In New Testament times, a kosher table defined identity and fellowship, making Jesus' table fellowship with tax collectors and sinners controversial. His ministry marked the end of the old object lessons of clean and unclean animals. Who would have thought that God would make such a big deal about eating? Leave it to our Creator to turn a simple meal into an object lesson of grace. 'There is no good trying to be more spiritual than God,' wrote C. S. Lewis in *Mere Christianity*. 'God never meant man to be a purely spiritual creature. That is why He uses material things like bread and wine to put the new life into us. We may think this rather crude and unspiritual. God does not: He invented eating. He likes matter. He invented it.'[2]

As Eugene Peterson has noted, 'It is striking how much of Jesus' life is told in settings defined by meals.'[3] We tend to talk about complex evangelistic strategies and techniques, but Jesus used simple hospitality and mealtime conversations to share the gospel. The question for us is this: how did Jesus befriend such a wide array of people *on their own turf*? How did He turn their hearts to the good news of God's grace over lunch? How did Jesus, who was 'homeless,' feel at home at a great banquet hosted by a tax collector named Levi and attended by a large crowd of his tax collector friends? How did Jesus, who was dirt poor, become the honored guest of a man by the name of Zacchaeus, who was filthy rich? The Pharisees may have called Jesus a glutton and a drunkard (Matt. 11:19), but they still invited Him for dinner, and He obliged them by telling parables with not-so-hidden meanings.

Jesus shared much of His ministry over meals. In the end, He invited His disciples to share the final meal with Him. This Last Supper, this eucharistic meal, is best observed in the household of faith, not with pomp and circumstance, but with the closest of connections to our ordinary, everyday life. The association between eating our daily bread and eating Christ's flesh and drinking His blood was close enough in the early church that they used the Jewish ritual of 'breaking bread' as a euphemism for celebrating Holy Communion (Acts 2:42). As Eugene Peterson reminds us, 'Our continuing witness to and fear-of-the-Lord participation in the work of salvation is formed eucharistically around our kitchen tables. Daily meals with

---

2   C. S. Lewis, *Mere Christianity* (San Francisco: HarperCollins, 2001), p. 64.

3   Eugene H. Peterson, *Christ Plays in Ten Thousand Places* (Grand Rapids: Eerdmans, 2005), p. 212.

family, friends and guests, acts of hospitality every one, are the most natural and frequent settings for working out the personal and social implications of salvation.'[4]

The two disciples on the road to Emmaus talked with the risen Lord Jesus, but they didn't recognize Him until He took bread, gave thanks, broke it, and began to give it to them. Likewise, we recognize the crucified and risen Lord best in the ordinary course of our daily lives. The apostle Paul's challenge remains, *'So here's what I want you to do, God helping you: Take your everyday, ordinary life—your sleeping, eating, going-to-work, and walking-around life— and place it before God as an offering'* (Rom. 12:1 MSG).

HOME HOSPITALITY

One Sunday in particular stands out for me as a wonderful experience of table fellowship. It gave me a taste of what the Great Banquet is going to be like. Following morning worship, our Sunday dinner took on the character of an early-church agape meal, the kind of table fellowship experienced by the church in Acts when they climaxed their dinner fellowship with Holy Communion. We have had many meals like this in our home, but this one was special. It was Easter, and out-of-town friends converged in San Diego. Earlier that day, we had met at church for worship. Eric flew in from D.C., Karen from Oregon, and close friends of our son, Chad and Kim, from Spokane, unexpectedly showed up at church that morning. In addition to this lively crew, our daughter Kennerly and her boyfriend Patrick had just announced their engagement. We were bound to have great fellowship with or without good food, but my wife Virginia outdid herself in preparing the meal: baked salmon topped with

---

4   Peterson, *Christ Plays in Ten Thousand Places* p. 214

sun-dried tomatoes, shallots, capers, and pine-nuts; wild rice; tossed salad with apples, cashews, and Cheddar cheese; and fresh bread.

In our house, setting the table for a special meal involves adding a leaf to the table, with a pressed tablecloth, folded napkins, plates and silverware properly placed. Virginia cuts some flowers and arranges a small centerpiece, careful not to obstruct anyone's view. Setting the table also involves relational work. People are befriended and invited. Food is purchased with the guests in mind and prepared specifically for them. In addition, spiritual preparation goes into the meal. What we bring to the table, whether it is joy or sadness, maturity or immaturity, has been in the works for some time leading up to the fellowship.

Before our noonday meal, we spent the morning in worship. We sang songs of praise and hymns. I preached on David's wilderness congregation, from 1 Samuel 22:2: 'And everyone who was in distress, and everyone who was in debt, and everyone who was bitter in soul, gathered to him. And he became captain over them.' The message focused on the providence, power, and grace of God in forming congregations and building ministry teams. David's motley congregation was compared to Jesus' team of Twelve and Paul's description of the local church at Corinth. The conclusion: God's great faithfulness goes before us, shaping community, nurturing fellowship, and inspiring service.

Good food. Great stories. In the company of lively saints, fellowship is charged with meaning. On the day I am recalling, there was plenty of laughter, sometimes even boisterous, especially at the end of the table where my wife was sitting. Conversational jazz is awesome: the extemporaneous improvisation of the soul. At the heart of table fellowship is a free-flowing banter that can jump from the sublime to the ridiculous, moving from the serious to the comedic.

Like a sports fan talking about a great play, Eric highlighted the morning worship experience. He compared the worship impact of the contemporary anthem 'Every Breath Is Yours' to Beethoven's 'Hallelujah Chorus.' He pulled his marked-up copy of the worship bulletin from his back pocket and summed up the message perfectly. From there our discussion went all over the map.

Lively saints produce lively yet unpretentious dialogue, free from one-upmanship. It may be edgy at times, but never cutting. Nothing fake. Everyone gets drawn in. Sincere questions. Real answers. This is a whole new experience for those raised on family meals filled with tension and berating. This is altogether different from the formal dinners where everything is about performing and impressing. Table fellowship may seem intimidating to those who grew up eating alone or in front of the TV, but it is worth the risk.

To bow in prayer and to break bread together is a eucharistic experience. This is because Christ is the real host, inviting us into His fellowship by His grace and mercy. The providence, power, and grace of God draw us into community. We bow and pray and pass the bread of life. We enjoy each other in Christ. Oftentimes, the benediction is unspoken as we part and go our separate ways into the world as salt and light and leaven.

I am not suggesting that all family meals are as meaningful as the one I am recalling. Perhaps it is their very rarity that makes them seem so special. It is not always possible to have friends and family together or to provide an elaborate meal for guests. Nevertheless, the principles of Christian hospitality are still in play, whether it is over a cup of coffee or a light meal shared on a lunch break.

Spirituality is often squeezed into a corner of life reserved for pious reflections and church services. But God intended spirituality to be at the center of our ordinary, everyday life together. Table grace refers to much more than the prayer at the beginning of a meal.

> Table grace is food for the mind, a metaphor for communion with God.
>
> Table grace is food for the body, a means for sustaining physical strength.
>
> Table grace is food for the soul, a method for understanding God's values.
>
> Table grace is food for the hungry, a model for serving Christ and His Kingdom.

The metaphor pictures the message; the means links body and soul in community; the method sets the strategy for holistic spirituality; and the model empowers the mission. Eating is serious business, but in a well-defined way.

Because of Christ's hospitality we have the opportunity to extend hospitality to others; to strangers and friends, to those who know Christ and to those who do not. In Christ, we learn that we need the fellowship of the needy if we are going to understand the hospitality of God's grace. God's invitation to us finds full expression in our invitation to others.

DISCUSSION:

1. How have you experienced this biblical theme of table grace in your life? When have you served as 'host' for others? When have you been another's 'guest'?

2. Why is it easy or difficult for you to talk about your faith in Christ over a meal? How do spiritual preparations factor into your practices of hospitality?

3. In what ways can you integrate true spirituality into your ordinary daily life?

4. How have you personally benefited from hospitality?

2

Setting the Table

You prepare a table before me in the presence of my enemies. You anoint my head with oil; my cup overflows.

Psalm 23:5

Whenever a meal is served somebody has to set the table, bake the bread, pour the wine, invite the guests, and host the meal. The Lord relishes this responsibility. We are invited to His table. To paraphrase the Song of Songs, 'He brought me to the banqueting house, and his banner over me is love' (Song 2:4). Table grace underscores the connection between our ordinary, everyday world and the grace of God in Christ. Thomas Howard writes:

> Holy things are ordinary things perceived in their true light, that is, as bearers of the divine mysteries and glory to us. Looked at in this way, eating becomes eucharistic, and working becomes the *opus dei* ('work of God'), and loving becomes an image of the City of God... We are set free to live in the splendor where eating and drinking and working and playing are known for what they really are: forms of perpetual worship and therefore bliss.[1]

---

1   Thomas Howard, *Splendor in the Ordinary: Your Home as a Holy Place* (Manchester, New Hampshire: Sophia Institute Press, 2000), p. 19.

From the start, the people of God have been encouraged to take their ordinary, Monday-thru-Friday world, with the weekend thrown in, and use it as a forum for spiritual direction. Following the most recognized call to worship in the Old Testament, 'Hear, O Israel: The LORD our God, the LORD is one. You shall love the LORD your God with all your heart and with all your soul and with all your might,' comes this command:

> 'And these words that I command you today shall be on your heart. You shall teach them diligently to your children, and shall talk of them when you sit in your house, and when you walk by the way, and when you lie down, and when you rise. You shall bind them as a sign on your hand, and they shall be as frontlets between your eyes. You shall write them on the doorposts of your house and on your gates' (Deut. 6:4-9).

Dr. Martin Luther King Jr. grew up in a home where table fellowship was important. His father was the pastor of Ebenezer Baptist Church in Atlanta, and Martin Luther King Sr. expected his children to come to the dinner table ready to share a Bible verse and a perspective on the day's news. Under his father's guidance, the ordinary family table was turned into a forum for spiritual direction and prayer.

Tradition posts a warning. This text can be misconstrued and spiritualized. The Pharisees had trouble reading metaphors and understanding what they meant. They took these commands literally and made phylacteries, little receptacles that contained biblical texts. They wrote out the text on parchment and placed these in two little boxes, one attached to the left arm near the heart and the other to the forehead. But, as Dale Bruner has pointed out,

'Ostentatious religion does not impress Jesus, for it uses God and the things of God for one's own honor.'[2]

The Pharisees envisioned a very different kind of spirituality than the real-world spirituality of Psalm 23. The psalmist pictures two images: the shepherd caring for his flock and the host caring for his friends. The scene changes from a beautiful pastoral landscape to a thanksgiving banquet. The modern reader may see the psalmist mixing his metaphors and juxtaposing two incompatible images, but to the Hebrew psalmist, steeped in wilderness pastoral imagery and the profound significance of the Passover feast, these two scenes blend beautifully. The shepherd with his flock and the host with his guests represent the natural, earth-tone beauty of God's care for us. King David describes ordinary life in the presence of God; a life filled with celebration, vindication, and exaltation, even in the course of daily life.

Only Christ's eucharistic meal does justice to the psalmist's imagery of the table prepared in the presence of our enemies. We are reminded of the fulfillment of the Passover imagery in the Good Shepherd who laid down His life for the sheep (John 10:11). We hear the voice of the prophet Isaiah saying, 'All we like sheep have gone astray; we have turned—every one—to his own way; and the LORD has laid on him the iniquity of us all. He was oppressed, and he was afflicted, yet he opened not his mouth; like a lamb that is led to the slaughter, and like a sheep that before its shearers is silent, so he opened not his mouth... He bore the sin of many, and makes intercession for the transgressors' (Isa. 53:6-7, 12). We hear the voice of the Savior saying, 'This is my body, which is given for you. Do

---

2   Frederick Dale Bruner, *Matthew: The Churchbook*, Vol. 2 (Grand Rapids: Eerdmans, 2004), p. 435.

this in remembrance of me.' And then he took the cup, saying, 'This cup that is poured out for you is the new covenant in my blood' (Luke 22:19-20). We were meant to read Psalm 23 in the light of the gospel of the Lord Jesus Christ.

Given the trajectory of salvation history, the phrase 'You prepare a table before me in the presence of my enemies' strikes us as an understatement. God the host became God the crucified in order to give us the hospitality we need for salvation. The preparation God had in mind involved an unimaginable cost, beyond all possible comparisons. Consider the most lavish state dinner: it is absolutely nothing next to God's table grace.

Six months of painstaking preparation is not uncommon for a full-course state dinner at Windsor Castle. No expense is spared. Every aspect of the royal event is planned in minute detail and orchestrated down to the minute. Hundreds of people are deployed in an event choreographed to perfection. Six different wine glasses for each of the several hundred dignitaries gives you some idea of the elaborate place setting. Customarily, the Queen arrives early to walk the length of the banquet hall, inspecting the table and giving her approval. During the banquet, all attention will be focused on the Queen, and everyone will follow her lead. Even though her role is largely ceremonial, to be in the presence of Her Majesty the Queen is an honor few, if any, would take lightly.

Now, imagine the shock that would ensue if the Queen broke with centuries of tradition and put on a servant's uniform and waited on her dinner guests. What if she who personified dignity and royalty became nothing more than one of the inconspicuous and anonymous waiters? What if, instead of presiding over the dinner, she served it? And then, what if—and this would only happen in our wildest dreams—the servant-queen became subject to accusation and abuse? What if she was scourged and crucified? But as shocking as this scenario sounds, it is nothing compared to God the host becoming God the crucified. In Psalm 23, the table in the presence of our enemies is a metaphor; the cross in the life of Jesus was not.

The images used to convey communion with God are not abstract concepts or lofty ideas or mystical feelings but down-to-earth word pictures that have a way of including us in David's vision for life in the presence of God. The images are not designed to indoctrinate or inform, but to invite participation in a relationship with the Lord.

Metaphor

Pictures provoke interest and raise questions. The 'table' in Psalm 23 is a metaphor, as is the head anointed with oil and the cup overflowing. These metaphors are useful in bridging the visible and the invisible worlds. They transpose truth into a key that we can understand and respond to. Metaphor is the language of sense experience used to lead us into the unseen world of redemption, faith, blessing, God. When Jesus said to His disciples, 'Take up your cross daily and follow me,' he was speaking metaphorically, not literally.

God has never literally set a table for me or anointed my head with oil or poured my cup to overflowing. We use metaphors because of the limits of language. Descriptive, revelatory language about God is always going to be inadequate and fall short. Some try hard to forsake metaphor and insist on pure thought, clear concepts, logical ideas, legal literalism. They are embarrassed because these metaphors lack the precision and logic that they are longing for. For them, the truth must be defined, explained, detailed, and packaged in precise propositions. But if that is the only way we speak and think, something is missing in our understanding of truth.

By their very nature, metaphors tend to be indirect and subtle. They refuse to spell out the meaning in pedantic prose or abstract concepts. They work their way into our thinking to form pictures rather than propositions. As Dale Bruner reminds us, 'The Word did not become a good idea, or a numinous feeling, or a moral aspiration: the Word became flesh and went on to change water into wine, and then wine into blood.'[3] The metaphors of Psalm 23 are personal and pastoral. Ordinary images are used to teach extraordinary truths. We are not 'gathering information or "doctrine" that we can study and use; we are residents in a home interpenetrated by spirit—God's Spirit, my spirit, your spirit. The metaphor makes us part of what we know.'[4]

The psalmist's metaphors are a form of literary hospitality, inviting us into the truth of God's redemptive love. The well-set table, the festive oil, and the brimming cup suggest a victory celebration. But these positive metaphors are not the whole story. Why did David add *in the presence of my enemies* to an otherwise peaceful and personal description of table fellowship? Why did he spoil the scene with enemy talk?

There are two short phrases in Psalm 23—the 'valley of the shadow of death' and 'in the presence of my enemies'—that grab our attention. They are striking metaphors for the harsh reality of pain and suffering experienced by us all. The psalmist puts hurt and hate in his picture of life. The metaphors do not spoil the picture; they connect the picture to reality. The spiritual life is not something that takes place in a sanctuary removed from the hassles and hostility of the world. David is

---

3   Frederick Dale Bruner, *Matthew: The Churchbook*, Vol. 2 p. 72.

4   Eugene H. Peterson, *Eat This Book: A Conversation in the Art of Spiritual Reading* (Grand Rapids: Eerdmans, 2006), p. 98.

not thinking here of a man's home being his castle, a fortified refuge walled off from his enemies. He's thinking of God's gracious provision in the midst of his enemies.

> You serve me a six-course dinner right in front of my enemies. You revive my drooping head; my cup brims with blessing. Your beauty and love chase after me every day of my life. I'm back home in the house of GOD for the rest of my life (Ps. 23:5-6, MSG).

The picture of the 'six-course dinner' may suggest that our enemies are envious of God's favor—we made God's guest list and they didn't. But that's not what David had in mind. It was not their envy, but his confidence in God that prompted his celebration. David knows that he can always count on God's provision, even in the presence of his enemies. To David, this is a picture of security and provision. He always has a home to come home to. 'I'm back home in the house of Yahweh for the rest of my life.'

King David's sense of overflowing celebration compares to the apostle Paul's unshakeable confidence. 'If God is for us,' declared Paul, 'who can be against us? He who did not spare his own Son but gave him up for us all, how will he not also with him graciously give us all things? . . . For I am sure that neither death nor life, nor angels nor rulers, nor things present nor things to come, nor powers, nor height nor depth, nor anything else in all creation, will be able to separate us from the love of God in Christ Jesus our Lord' (Rom. 8:31-32, 38-9).

The psalm ends on a bright, positive picture of a journey through life that has been blessed by the Lord from start to finish. It is a reminder to us that our true home awaits us. Our true home is not where we are from but where we are headed. Jesus said, 'Let not your hearts be troubled. Believe in God; believe also in me ... If I go and prepare a place for you, I will come again and will take you to myself, that where I am you may be also ... I am the way, and the truth, and the life. No one comes to the Father except through me' (John 14:1-6).

In six verses of everyday language and common images, Psalm 23 captures the simplicity, beauty, and depth of a personal relationship with the living God. Christians tend to link Psalm 23 with John 10. The shepherd psalm is fulfilled in Jesus' declaration, 'I am the good shepherd. The good shepherd lays down his life for the sheep' (John 10:11). But Christians may also link Psalm 23 to John 2, the story of Jesus' first miracle. The table fellowship envisioned in Psalm 23 is fulfilled in Jesus the host, who turns water to wine. When we read these passages together, the meaning of the psalm and the witness of the gospel converge. The unifying story of the Bible as a whole is brought out. One part echoes and enriches the other.

Miracle
History began with a wedding (Gen. 2) and will climax with the Marriage Supper of the Lamb. 'Let us rejoice and exult and give him the glory, for the marriage of the Lamb has come, and his Bride has made herself ready' (Rev. 19:7). Jesus also began His earthly ministry blessing a wedding — more specifically, at a wedding feast. Jesus was at the party as an ordinary guest, but before it was over he was serving as the host (Luke 7:31-35). The wedding celebration became a messianic celebration. Jesus revealed His glory 'and his disciples believed in him' (John 2:11).

In the wedding feast of Cana, wine is a symbol of joy and celebration, and its absence provoked a behind-the-scenes crisis. C. S. Lewis described the miracle of changing water to wine as a miracle of the old creation.

The fitness of the Christian miracles ... lies in the fact that they show invasion by a Power which is not alien... Each miracle writes for us in small letters something that God has already written, or will write, in letters almost too large to be noticed, across the whole canvas of Nature ... Every year as part of the Natural order, God makes wine. He does so by creating a vegetable organism that can turn water, soil, and sunlight into a juice which will, under proper conditions, become wine ... Once, and in one year only, God, now incarnate, short circuits the process: makes wine in a moment ... The Miracle consists in the short cut; but the event to which it leads is the usual one.[5]

MESSIAH

The master of the wedding banquet was impressed. He took the bridegroom aside and said, 'Everyone serves the good wine first, and when people have drunk freely, then the poor wine. But you have kept the good wine until now' (John 2:10). The world's parties never measure up to the table fellowship provided by Jesus. Changing water to wine is a sign of things to come, introducing the new wine that will break old wineskins. As Jesus said, 'No one puts new wine into old wineskins. If he does, the wine will burst the skins—and the wine is destroyed, and so are the skins. But new wine is for fresh wineskins' (Mark 2:22).

The wedding at Cana is a symbol of messianic fulfillment (Rev. 19:9). An abundance of wine (120 gallons) is a symbol for the joy of the final days: the reception to end all receptions, the Marriage Supper of the Lamb. 'Write this: Blessed are those who are invited to the wedding supper of the Lamb!' (Rev. 19:9). We could not attend the wedding

---

5   C. S. Lewis, *Miracles* (New York: Macmillan, 1947), pp. 137, 141.

at Cana, but Jesus invites us to another, more spectacular wedding.

Jesus literally turned water into wine, and in John 6, He speaks metaphorically of turning wine into blood. Only the Marriage Supper of the Lamb promises to fulfill the symbolism conveyed by changing water to wine at the wedding feast. Only Christ's eucharistic meal does justice to the psalmist's imagery of the table prepared 'in the presence of my enemies.' God's table grace extends from daily bread to the Bread of Life. The Lord has set a table for us and He invites us into His presence, but it is up to us to respond to His invitation. Surely the Lord does not force us to eat with Him, but who would turn down such hospitality?

DISCUSSION:

1. Psalm 23 presents two important images: the shepherd caring for his flock and the host caring for his friends. Which image portrays for you a greater intimacy? What does it mean for you to be at home with the Lord?

2. The well-set table, the festive oil, and the brimming cup suggest a victory celebration. Why did David add to his description *in the presence of my enemies*? Why spoil the scene with enemy talk? Who or what are we up against?

3. Jesus' first week of public ministry climaxed at a wedding feast where He turned water into wine. How does this miracle make us think back to the first week of creation and forward to the Marriage Supper of the Lamb?

4. If God sets the table for us, how can we set the table for others?

3

A Working Lunch

I [will] bring a morsel of bread, that you may refresh
yourselves, and after that you may pass on—since
you have come to your servant.

Genesis 18:5

Narratives do not spell out things the way many sermons
do. Good stories plant a seed. They leave an impression.
They don't work things into a formula and package the
truth for easy consumption. When Moses wrote up God's
working lunch with Abraham, he didn't reduce it to three
bullet points. Instead, he crafted his true story to show
how God related to Abraham. The encounter between
God and Abraham remains meaningful on two levels.
First, it demonstrates the down-to-earth, personal way in
which God encountered Abraham. Second, it models the
way the gospel can be shared today. Then and now, lunch
becomes the occasion for the divine encounter. The gospel works into the daily routines of life. The way the story
of the covenant unfolds here works as 'a protest against
theology depersonalized into information about God; it is
a protest against theology functionalized into a program of
strategic planning for God.'[1]

---

1   Eugene H. Peterson, *Christ Plays In Ten Thousand Places*, p. 1.

Moses introduced this incredible encounter with a simple factual line: 'The LORD appeared to Abraham' (Gen. 18:1, NIV). This line defines the meaning of the moment, but leaves the circumstances of the encounter to play in our imagination. Up until now, we have been told that the Lord speaks to Abraham, but nothing is said about how the Lord speaks to him (Gen. 12:1; 13:14; 15:1). After the birth of Ishmael, the Lord appeared to Abraham to renew His covenant and reaffirm His promise. Abraham's reaction is described: he fell face down before the Lord. But the circumstances of the encounter are not given.

In this next encounter the mystery remains, but the circumstances of the meeting are described. Abraham is the Lord's host. God is the recipient of hospitality. Abraham is camped out at his favorite spot, located near the great trees of Mamre outside Hebron. He is sitting at the entrance to his tent in the heat of the day. The scene intentionally juxtaposes Abraham's ordinary daily routine with his extraordinary encounter with God. We are drawn into the story with a mental picture of what this scene may have looked like, but the three visitors remain something of an enigma. We are never told how Abraham knew the identity of this delegation. Abraham's actions are easy to describe, but the appearance of the Lord is shrouded in mystery.

This true story illustrates not only biblical hospitality, but the way in which God shared the gospel with Abraham. The storyteller pictures Abraham as the ideal host. He is open, inviting, eager, practical, efficient, and caring; all the things you look for in a good host. Our first glimpse of Abraham, the host, is of him sitting 'at the door of his tent in the heat of the day.' Good hospitality begins with waiting. We will never be open to God or anyone else if we are always in a hurry and insisting on control. Waiting increases expectation and prepares the heart for hospitality. Sitting at the entrance of his tent, Abraham is hardly a picture of drivenness. He's open, ready for an interruption.

Learning how to wait is usually not a priority for busy Americans. We can hardly imagine what Abraham's life was like without all the electronic devices we use to stay connected and distracted. No iPod cord in his ear, no cell phone on his belt, and no laptop at his fingers. Abraham was able to be 'interrupted' because he was waiting and available. Pastor Mark Buchanan observes, 'Think a moment of all the events and encounters that have shaped you most deeply and lastingly. How many did you see coming? How many did you engineer, manufacture, chase down? And how many were interruptions?'[2]

In his classic little piece on Christian community, *Life Together*, Dietrich Bonhoeffer writes:

> We must be ready to allow ourselves to be interrupted by God. God will be constantly crossing our paths and canceling our plans by sending us people with claims and petitions... It is part of the discipline of humility that we must not spare our hand where it can perform a service and that we do not assume our schedule is our own to manage, but allow it to be arranged by God.[3]

Being busy and learning how to wait on God are not incompatible spiritual disciplines. Some of the busiest people I know have cultivated a deep sensitivity to God's

---

2   Mark Buchanan, 'Schedule, Interrupted,' *Christianity Today*, February, 2, 2006.

3   Dietrich Bonhoeffer, *Life Together* (San Francisco: HarperCollins, 1954), p. 99.

timely interruptions. When Dr. Vernon Grounds was president of Denver Theological Seminary, he impressed so many of us with his willingness to stop what he was doing and spend time with all sorts of people. In the midst of his rigorous schedule, there was a deep current of rest and peace that made him available to others. 'Busy' is probably not the right word to describe a person like Dr. Grounds who is practicing the rhythms of grace. Like Abraham, such people are hard-working, diligent, and productive, but by the grace of God they have disciplined themselves to be ready for what God has in store for them in the course of their day.

Good hospitality is more intuitive than calculated. '[Abraham] lifted up his eyes and looked, and behold, three men were standing in front of him.' (Gen. 18:2) Hospitality always precedes friendship. Someone has to take a risk. Abraham sees these three men as potential guests, not unwelcome enemies. He begins the encounter with trust, not suspicion. The world is not out to get Abraham, but Abraham is out to befriend the world.

HOSPITALITY

Good hospitality is humble. 'When he saw them, he ran from the tent door to meet them and bowed himself to the earth.' He intuitively sensed that these men were important, but I'm not sure he grasped *how* important. Abraham related to these three strangers with a certain awe and circumspection proper to all beings made in God's image. As C.S. Lewis says so well, 'There are no ordinary people. You have never talked to a mere mortal... Next to the Blessed Sacrament itself, your neighbor is the holiest object presented to your senses.'[4] If this is our

---

4   C. S. Lewis, *The Weight of Glory* (New York: Collier Books, 1980), p. 19.

starting point with people, we will never go wrong. Instead of insisting that people need to prove their value by who they know or what they have done, we will accept them as image-bearers of God. We will welcome them even as Christ has welcomed us.

Good hospitality is eager. In the noonday heat, Abraham exerted himself. He ran to meet his guests and then hurried into the tent to get Sarah. 'Quick,' he said. 'Get the flour. Start baking.' He ran to the herd, selected a calf, and got a servant to quickly prepare it. Then he provided appetizers while they waited for the main course. Imagine Abraham and Sarah experiencing the same adrenaline rush and slightly frazzled feeling you experience when you are scurrying around trying to get ready for guests.

Good hospitality is extravagant. Abraham attended to his guests' unspoken needs. He played down his offering: 'Let a little water be brought, and wash your feet, and rest yourselves under the tree, while I bring a morsel of bread, that you may refresh yourselves...' (Gen. 18:4-5). But he pulled out all the stops on his generosity: Thirty-six pounds of fine flour, a choice, tender calf, and the finest yogurt. He gave his guests the best he had. Recently, good friends invited my wife and me to one of the best French restaurants in New York City. The food, the ambience, and the bill were by all standards extravagant! But that is not the kind of extravagance Abraham demonstrated here. His hospitality was not a matter of quantitative abundance as much as a generous attentiveness to the needs of his guests. Good hospitality is extravagant in that it involves giving the best that we have, no matter how much or little that might be.

Good hospitality follows the principle of the exchanged life. 'And he stood by them under the tree while they ate.' In practical ways, Abraham practiced the 'My-Life-For-

Yours' principle. True excitement for fellowship with God is born of expectation, exertion, and humility. Abraham greeted this encounter with the Lord with great eagerness. To wait hand and foot on his three guests, whose identities are shrouded in mystery, is his high honor. This story 'has entered the Christian imagination as a defining moment for hospitality as Trinitarian presence.'[5]

One of church history's leading theological voices, Augustine, paid careful attention to Genesis 18. He claimed that this passage of Scripture demanded 'neither slight nor passing consideration.'[6] His instincts were good. He was unwilling to skip over this text and conclude that it was just an example of good storytelling. Struck by the paradox of the three men and one Lord, Augustine asked whether it was one person of the Trinity that appeared to Abraham or 'God Himself the Trinity.'[7] Instead of ignoring the fact that Abraham entertained three men yet spoke to one Lord, Augustine reflected on its significance. He reasoned that 'since three men appeared, and no one of them is said to be greater than the rest either in form, or age, or power, why should we not here understand, as visibly intimated by the visible creature, the equality of the Trinity, and one and the same substance in three persons?'[8] Mystery surrounds the identity of these three strangers, and Abraham's eager hospitality was meant to impress us.

Augustine felt his conclusion was confirmed by the fact that when the three parted company, the one who

5 Eugene H. Peterson, *Christ Plays In Ten Thousand Places*, p. 212.

6 Augustine, *On The Trinity, Nicene and Post-Nicene Fathers*, Vol. 3, Book II, Chap. 11, Sec. 20, (Peabody, Massachusetts: Hendrickson Publishers, 1995), p. 47.

7 Ibid., p. 45.

8 Ibid., p. 47

remained behind to talk to Abraham was addressed as 'Lord,' while the other two who went down to see Lot were also addressed as 'Lord' (19:18). Textual critics solve the paradox by reading a plural form of 'lords,' but Augustine was not so easily dissuaded from seeing the mystery of the triune God in the divine appearances to Abraham and Lot.

> Are we here, too, to understand two persons in the plural number, but when the two are addressed as one, then the one Lord God of one substance? But which two persons do we here understand?—of the Father and of the Son, or of the Father and of the Holy Spirit, or of the Son and of the Holy Spirit? The last, perhaps, is the more suitable; for they said of themselves that they were sent, which is that which we say of the Son and of the Holy Spirit. For we find nowhere in the Scriptures that the Father was sent.[9]

Augustine was not dogmatic on this point, but neither did he dismiss the story as 'an unreflective account of a revelatory disclosure.'[10] If the choice is between a playful, imaginative text or the mystery of God's own self-disclosure, I would side with Augustine's sober conclusion that God is coming to Abraham in the fullness of His personal being. And the manner of His coming is suggestive of what has already been disclosed (see Gen. 1:26) and what will be more fully disclosed in the course of salvation history. We are made in God's image and destined for fellowship with Him and with each other.

The strangeness of this encounter is heightened by how the story is told. The Lord appeared to Abraham 'by

---

9   Augustine, *On The Trinity, Nicene and Post-Nicene Fathers*, Vol. 3, Book II, Chap. 11, Sec. 20, p. 48.

10   Walter Brueggemann, *Genesis* (Atlanta: John Knox Press, 1982), p. 158.

the oaks of Mamre, as he sat at the door of his tent in the heat of the day.' But when he looked up, he saw 'three men were standing in front of him.' This narrative juxtaposition describes the appearance of the Lord as a three-man visit. Abraham ran to meet them and 'bowed himself to the earth.' His eagerness seems to exceed even Ancient Near Eastern custom and heightens the sense that this is a highly unusual encounter. Strangely, there appears to be no hierarchy among the three. If one of them was the Lord, we would expect some differentiation. Yet when Abraham addresses them, he does not speak to three lords but to one Lord. 'O Lord (or, 'my Lord'), if I have found favor in your sight, do not pass by your servant.' We would expect the Lord to respond, but the answer Abraham receives comes from the group and not anyone in particular. 'So they said, "Do as you have said"'.

CONVERSATION

The Lord came to Abraham to establish and renew His promise in four significant ways. The promise was that God had chosen him and his descendants as the people through whom God would bless the nations. Each time the Lord reaffirmed this promise, the relationship grew more personal. There was a relational progression from the call (12:1-8) to the covenant (15:1-21), and from the circumcision (17:1-27) to the conversation (18:1-15). After the three men ate, the Lord spoke to Abraham and promised him that Sarah would have a son in about a year. From the narrative, we picture Abraham hovering over his guests, anxious to please them in every way. It is a poignant reminder that the Lord of the universe and the God of the covenant desires to be up close and personal with us. Our God is a relational God, and the only way we truly know ourselves is in relation to God. Just as we cannot find ourselves apart from relating to God, we cannot be ourselves apart from relating to others.

The author of Genesis contrasts Abraham and Lot. Abraham sat at the entrance to his tent under the trees of Mamre, and Lot sat at the gateway of the city of Sodom. Abraham was ready and able to offer good hospitality. He was the consummate host. But Lot, while willing and eager, lived in a situation that made genuine hospitality: impossible. Lot chose a way of life hostile to hospitality. He probably didn't mean to do that, but he did. Choices were made that ruined his ability to show hospitality. Abraham's royal banquet is compared to Lot's provision of unleavened bread (Gen. 19:3).

Over a meal, God shares the news with Abraham that the Lord is the Promise-Keeper. The occasion may have been the first of its kind, but the picture will be repeated over and over again. It points forward to Jesus breaking bread with the disciples in the upper room and revealing His identity to the disciples from Emmaus after the Resurrection. This is the same Lord who promises, 'Behold, I stand at the door and knock. If anyone hears my voice and opens the door, I will come in to him and eat with him, and he with me' (Rev. 3:20).

Isaac embodied the promise that God made to Abraham, that He would make him into a great nation and bless all peoples on earth through him (Gen. 12:2-3). It is evident from the beginning that God determined to work personally through Abraham and Sarah's family to bring about our redemption. God didn't choose lone individuals to push His agenda or to lead a crusade, but a family, followed by a family of families, through whom to bless 'all peoples on earth.' God's redemptive strategy was not just a line of biological descendants, but a promise-keeping people who chose to place their trust in 'the Father, from whom every family in heaven and on earth is named' (Eph. 3:14-15). Salvation history is a relational history of families placing their trust in the personal God who promises to bless all those who trust in Him and reconcile them to Himself. So we see in retrospect that Isaac represented the coming Incarnate One, just as we see the interpersonal nature of the triune God who revealed Himself to Abraham.

Kent Hughes writes, 'This is the only place in Scripture before the Incarnation that the Lord ate a meal with a human being ... The meal with Abraham was an exercise of spiritual intimacy. To dine with Yahweh at the table was and is the ultimate honor any mortal could have in this world.'[11] The next covenantal meal will be the Passover (Exod. 24:5).

Good hospitality always draws people in and then draws them out. 'Where is Sarah your wife?' they asked him. Then the Lord invited Sarah into the conversation. An eavesdropping Sarah overheard their conversation. She heard the promise and laughed to herself. The mystery of the relationship between three men and one Lord is overshadowed, if you can imagine, by the Lord's inquiry into Sarah's laughter. In a touching way, the Lord proved Himself to Sarah. God took her seriously. 'Why did Sarah laugh and say, "Shall I indeed bear a child, now that I am old?" Is anything too hard for the LORD?' Sarah's reaction was to lie. 'I did not laugh,' she protested. But the Lord said, 'No, but you did laugh.' When you think about it, it was an amazing exchange between Sarah and the Lord over the family that would bless the nations. God wanted Sarah to be in on the promise.

---

11   R. Kent Hughes, *Genesis: Beginning and Blessing* (Wheaton, Illinois: Crossway, 2004), p. 254.

In On the Promise

The conversation between the Lord and Sarah reminds me of an occasion many years ago when Virginia and I invited several visiting biblical scholars to our home for lunch. Virginia had prepared a special lunch, and everyone was hungry after a long morning of teaching. The table talk was intense and serious. Our guests talked mainly about their work and academic life. Two of the scholars pretty much ignored Virginia. They treated her like a restaurant waitress putting on a meal. The one exception was the well-known theologian and author J. I. Packer. He related to my wife as if she were a full participant in the conversation. He asked about our children and shared about his family. He expressed gratitude for the meal and paid attention to the host. Packer wanted Virginia to be in on the conversation.

In the Genesis story, we are aware that the Lord wanted Sarah to be in on the promise and, by God's grace, she became part of the conversation. We want to follow the Lord's lead in drawing others into the conversation. Good conversation requires a measure of selflessness. Most of us have to learn to cultivate the art of engaging others in meaningful dialogue, because it doesn't come naturally. We have to work at it, pray about it, and make it a matter of spiritual discernment. It is all too easy to sit there and let the conversation languish on the mundane matters of weather and gossip, especially among our own family members. Why is it that we make such an effort to engage colleagues and clients in conversation, but then become dull and boring around the people we love the most?

Good conversationalists pay attention to others. They are not experts in small talk, but students of people. They read their listeners carefully, and their table talk has purpose. They seek to love and learn from others *with all wisdom.* They care enough to communicate what they mean to say accurately and thoughtfully. They are not oversensitive or easily offended. One of the most natural opportunities we have for expressing the fruit of the Spirit is mealtime conversation (see Gal. 5:22-23). The Lord showed His love for Sarah by including her in the conversation.

The narrative resumes with the three men getting up to leave and looking toward Sodom, but the story adds a significant development. It reports a conversation that the Lord had within Himself. Instead of addressing Abraham directly, the Lord talks about him. Is this a question between the three, or an internal dialogue within the Lord? Perhaps we were not meant to distinguish between the three and the one. The disclosure of God's own decision-making is revealing:

> Shall I hide from Abraham what I am about to do, seeing that Abraham shall surely become a great and mighty nation, and all the nations of the earth shall be blessed in him? For I have chosen him, that he may command his children and his household after him to keep the way of the LORD by doing righteousness and justice, so that the LORD may bring to Abraham what he has promised him (Gen. 18:17-19).

The fact that the Lord deliberated over disclosing to Abraham what He planned to do about Sodom is significant. A distinctive pattern of meaningful disclosure was being established by the Lord. In order for Abraham to direct his family in the way of the Lord, he had to be brought into dialogue with the Lord. This moment is decisive and reveals a pattern of God's self-disclosure throughout salvation history.

The Lord wants us in on the promise too. The Lord wants us in the know. God keeps coming to us on our home turf to make His home with us. The foundational truth for Christian hospitality is that 'the Word became flesh and dwelt among us, and we have seen his glory, glory as of the only Son from the Father, full of grace and truth' (John 1:14). God bridges the cultures, crosses the boundaries, ignores the barriers, and makes His way into our lives.

In that same Spirit, we are called to go out of our way to extend hospitality. The author of Hebrews writes, 'Let brotherly love continue. Do not neglect to show hospitality to strangers...' (Heb. 13:1-2). In the parable of the sheep and the goats, Jesus made it clear that by feeding the hungry and inviting the stranger in, we are ministering to Him— we are extending hospitality to the Lord God. 'Truly, I say to you, as you did it to one of the least of these my brothers and sisters, you did it to me' (Matt. 25:40).

Abraham and Sarah's daily work of hosting a meal, living by faith in the promise and bearing a child is juxtaposed with the eternal saving work of God. Like them, we are invited to participate in salvation history in the ordinary course of daily faithfulness and obedience. The promise of the gospel was meant to be shared around the table. Christian hospitality is the way our children, friends, relatives, and neighbors were meant to hear the gospel. Eugene Peterson laments the loss of the family meal:

> The practice of hospitality has fallen on bad times. Fewer and fewer families sit down to a meal together. The meal, which used to be a gathering place for families, neighbors, and 'the stranger at the gate,' is on its way out... A primary, maybe the primary, venue for evangelism in Jesus' life was

the meal. Is Jesus' preferred setting for playing out the work of salvation on this field of history only marginally available to us?[12]

The early church spread the gospel from house to house. The table was their pulpit (Acts 5:42; 20:20). If we follow their example, we will add lunch to the liturgy.

DISCUSSION:

1. Over a working lunch, the Lord shared His plans with Abraham and Sarah. What made this table fellowship especially significant?

2. Why do you think the storyteller sets the scene in such detail, but shrouds the three guests in mystery?

3. How does the Lord invite our hospitality today? Do we face similar opportunities today? See Heb. 13:1-2 and Matt. 25:34-46.

4. How does the Lord share His work with us? Are we as eager as Abraham to hear the news and participate in the promise? How can we cultivate openness to God's work in the midst of the distractions of modern life?

---

12   Eugene H. Peterson, *Christ Plays in Ten Thousand Places*, p. 214.

4

Table Manners

...When you give a feast, invite the poor, the crippled, the lame, the blind, and you will be blessed, because they cannot repay you. For you will be repaid at the resurrection of the just.

Luke 14:13-14

We look to Jesus for our table manners, and as you might suspect, we're not referring to Emily Post's mealtime manners. The etiquette of place settings and what you may or may not eat with your fingers doesn't concern us here. We want to think about Jesus' Kingdom ethic. We shouldn't be surprised that His Kingdom customs are very different from the world's. Fellowship in the world is often based on self-importance, but Jesus' fellowship is based on self-sacrifice. The principle of the exchanged life, my life for yours, remains the hallmark of Jesus' table grace. The principle of the expendable life, your life for mine, is frequently the force behind the world's social status. But the principle of the cross, my life for yours, empowers Christian hospitality.

Consider the difference between a banquet sponsored by the world and a banquet hosted by the Lord. The poor, weak, lame, and sick are invited to Jesus' table, but the status-seeking, self-important social climbers are not. Those who are proud of their accomplishments and looking for recognition are excluded, and those who are aware of their tremendous need for God are included.

Some things money can't buy, and table grace is one of them. Formal banquets in expensive hotels are usually not all that fun. Seating is cramped and conversation stilted. Because of the din of background noise, you often have to shout to be heard across the table. Everyone seems a bit awkward and not quite themselves. I'd prefer a good conversation with a friend, a turkey sandwich on sourdough and a pitcher of iced tea, to an expensive dinner entrée hurriedly plopped down by a waiter who is scurrying around trying to serve too many tables. Fund-raising banquets are the worst. Staging an expensive meal in a posh hotel to attract donors seems to violate the very spirit of hospitality.

Fund-raising banquets remind me of a humorous greeting card that I found in a gift shop. It caught my attention because it used my surname, but it struck me as funny because of its caricature of life. The card pictures two vultures perched in their nest on the face of a cliff overlooking the desert. One of them is on the phone, and turns to the other, saying, 'It's the Websters. They say there's some pitiful thing dying of thirst out their way, and would we like to come over?' Vultures have to eat too.

The prominent Pharisee who invited Jesus to dinner on the Sabbath was acting more like a circling vulture than a gracious host. He used hospitality as a convenient way to scrutinize Jesus. Dinner was a set-up, and Jesus was the prey. Luke's description of the Pharisee as 'prominent' suggests a negative assessment (Luke 14:1, NIV). 'Prominence' is a dangerous classification, because it alludes to self-importance. It implies the criticism Jesus leveled against the Pharisees when he said, 'Woe to you, scribes and Pharisees, hypocrites! For you shut the kingdom of heaven in people's faces. For you neither enter yourselves nor allow those who would enter to go in' (Matt. 23:13-14).

The Pharisees and the experts in the law formed an inner circle, and there was little question in their minds that Jesus was on the outside. They were proud of their exclusiveness and confident that the boundary they had drawn around themselves was a righteous one. They imagined that Jesus wanted in, that He needed their approval and sought their accreditation. They had counted up what it had cost them to belong to this exclusive religious club, and they were not about to extend privileges to this nonconformist teacher without rigorous scrutiny. 'There'd be no fun if there were no outsiders,' writes C. S. Lewis. 'The invisible line would have no meaning unless most people were on the wrong side of it. Exclusion is no accident; it is the essence.'[1] But they have it all wrong. Jesus flips their world. He exposes the self-righteous insiders as outsiders and the needy God-dependent outsiders as the true insiders. God's hospitality turns everything upside down.

No one deserves to be watched more than Jesus, but in the Pharisee's home, the scrutiny was for all the wrong reasons. The group watched Jesus with a jaundiced eye, while Jesus looked with compassion on a man who needed help. Luke describes the encounter this way: 'Right before him there was a man hugely swollen in his joints' (Luke 14:2 MSG). On the Sabbath, in the home of a Pharisee, Jesus is presented with a person in need of healing. It looks to me like the spiritually bloated had set up a sting operation to see if Jesus would violate their Sabbath laws. Hostility masqueraded as hospitality.

---

1   C. S. Lewis, *The Weight of Glory: The Inner Ring* (New York: Macmillan, 1980), p. 104.

TENSION AROUND THE TABLE

There must have been considerable tension around that table. When Jesus asked, 'Is it lawful to heal on the Sabbath, or not?' they remained silent. Jesus refused to treat the suffering man as an object lesson. He quickly healed the man and sent him on his way. Then Jesus asked, 'Which of you, having a son or an ox that has fallen into a well on a Sabbath day, will not immediately pull him out?' Again, they were silent. They had nothing to say. What a strange and awkward meal it must have been.

We may think that the real problem between people is a lack of communication. If we could only dialogue more, then our problems would disappear. But the dialogue between Jesus and the Pharisees only proved how far apart they really were. The Pharisees were 'lying in wait for him, to catch him in something he might say' (Luke 11:54), but Jesus turned the tables and silenced His accusers. He scrutinized the scrutinizers. He called them on their habit of picking out places of honor for themselves by telling them a story. In Jesus' story, an unlucky guest picked out a seat at the head table only to be embarrassingly removed by somebody more important. This scenario illustrates the humiliating dangers of self-importance and echoes Solomon's proverb: 'Do not put yourself forward in the king's presence or stand in the place of the great, for it is better to be told, "Come up here," than to be put lower in the presence of a noble' (Prov. 25:6-7).

Jesus' companions at dinner that day did not have the faintest idea in whose presence they were jockeying for preferred seating, but we do. As Jesus looked on, they revealed their true self-serving selves. The same thing happens to us. When we seek privilege and praise, Jesus, the King of kings, is observing. The bottom line of the parable he told that day is clear: Don't do this. Don't be this way. Don't seek your own glory at the expense of others. 'For everyone who exalts himself will be humbled, and he who humbles himself will be exalted' (Luke 14:11).

In the Bible, humility and humiliation stand as opposites. Humility is a spiritual discipline, an intentional commitment of the will in relationship to God and others. It is a chosen and cultivated quality of character that matures and deepens with our experience in Christ. Humility is a surrender of our will to the commands of God and the needs of others. The apostle's exhortation, 'Have this mind among yourselves, which is yours in Christ Jesus,' calls for an intentional and resolute self-emptying (Phil. 2:5). Humility is the chosen awareness of our needy dependence on the mercy and wisdom of God. Humiliation is the feeling of shame, inadequacy, and disappointment that comes from our own sinful self-reliance. Humiliation involves trusting in ourselves; humility involves trusting in God. Humiliation rejects God; humility bows before God. Humiliation leads to despair; humility leads to hope. Humiliation thrives on self-promotion; humility frees us from the pressure to make a name for ourselves. Humiliation is our enemy, we feel it in our soul; but humility is our friend, whether we know it or not. For there is no other way to deal with humiliation, than with humility.

At dinner with Jesus that day, humility was not on display. The tension at the table grew greater. Jesus was now in charge of the conversation, and I imagine the Pharisees had lost their appetite. Imagine the keynote speaker at a banquet observing publicly that all the wrong people had been invited. Jesus was neither indirect nor subtle. 'When you give a dinner or a banquet, do not invite your friends...' I picture the prominent Pharisee, with an angry face, saying to himself, 'Who gives him the right to say this in my house?!' The message was insulting. Jesus was lecturing them on hospitality—on the kingdom ethic. Instead of inviting their well-heeled friends, Jesus told them to invite 'the poor, the crippled, the lame, the blind, and you will be blessed.'

Someone at the table attempted to rescue the moment. He offered a well-meaning, pious platitude: 'Blessed is everyone who will eat bread in the kingdom of God!' I suspect that the guest's purpose for speaking up was to smooth over the tension that Jesus had created. The benediction was meant to wrap up things on a positive note. But Jesus wasn't finished. The situation called for a different and less friendly conclusion. Neither the polite setting nor a pious saying controlled the conversation.

Truth at the table is just as important as truth from the pulpit and the lectern. Instead of gossip or small talk, Jesus launches into the parable of the great banquet. His intent was to correct a theological misunderstanding. The Pharisees thought they were the quintessential insiders, but Jesus warned them that if they did not receive His invitation, they would be on the outside. No matter how prominent a Pharisee might be, if he refused to enter through the narrow door, he would be left out of the kingdom of God.

Luke meant for us to read Jesus' parable in response to the person who asked, 'Lord, will those who are saved be few?' (Luke 13:23). Jesus sets the tone for a series of inclusion/exclusion conversations with the image of the narrow door. 'Strive to enter through the narrow door. For many, I tell you, will seek to enter and will not be able' (Luke 13:24). Jesus pictured the people on the outside knocking and pleading with the owner of the house, saying, 'Lord, open to us.' When the owner refuses to open the door, they complain, 'We ate and drank in your presence, and you taught in our streets.' But the homeowner said, 'I tell you, I do not know where you come from.'

The parable of the great banquet continues and completes this earlier discussion. Those who miss the feast with lame excuses are like those clamoring to get in after the door is closed. Jesus encourages people to make every effort to enter through the narrow door. The people in the parable are pretty laid-back and casual about attending the great banquet. They are not only *not* making any effort—they are snubbing the host! 'They make polite excuses but the excuses are transparently thin. They could come if they wished: they have no wish to come.'[2]

Howard Marshall writes concerning this passage: 'All three excuses are concerned with the details of commercial and family life, and fit in with the teaching of Jesus regarding the danger of letting love of possessions or domestic ties interfere with total commitment to the call to discipleship; they do not need to be allegorized in order to be interpreted outside the parable.'[3] Helmut Thielicke notes,

> As a rule, the road to hell is paved not with crimes and great scandals but with things that are quite harmless, with pure proprieties, and simply because these harmless proprieties acquire a false importance in our life, because they suddenly get in our light... They still refused to take the risk of accepting that great joy and giving up their own indulgences and ties in order to have it.[4]

---

2   David Gooding, *According to Luke* (Grand Rapids: Eerdmans, 1987), p. 268.

3   I. Howard Marshall, *New International Greek Testament Commentary: The Gospel of Luke* (Grand Rapids: Eerdmans, 1978), p. 588.

4   Helmut Thielicke, *The Waiting Father: Sermons on the Parables of Jesus* (New York: Harper & Brothers, 1959), p. 186.

If we stop and think about it, we can find ourselves in these polite and seemingly innocent excuses. We have our own agenda, and we expect God to conform to our wish-dream expectations. David Goetz explores the toxic good life in *Death by Suburb*. As much as we might not like to admit it, there is a link between suburban, middle-class Christians and the prominent Pharisees in dinner conversation with Jesus. Well-intentioned believers have so many options and distractions that compete with the 'narrow door' invitation to follow Jesus. Goetz argues that 'the suburbs tend to produce inverse spiritual cripples.'[5] In a suburban environment of security, efficiency, and opportunities, the over-indulged self reduces spirituality to yet another program designed to get people involved and busier than ever. 'Too much of the good life ends up being toxic, deforming us spiritually. The drive to succeed, to make one's children succeed, overpowers the best intentions to live more reflectively, no matter the piety. Should it be any surprise that the true life in Christ never germinates?'[6]

Reversing our excuse-prone suburban lifestyle begins with embracing God's invitation. There is nothing really complicated about saying 'yes' to Jesus' invitation to 'come.' And if you envision yourself honestly accepting Jesus' invitation to the Great Banquet, perhaps you could begin by embracing the spiritual discipline of table fellowship, by carving out enough time with family, friends, and neighbors to eat together and pray together. The simple practice of breaking bread together, reading a chapter of the Bible out loud, and praying together will do wonders for your soul. We need not make this complicated. The Holy Spirit

5   David Goetz, *Death by Suburb: How To Keep The Suburbs From Killing Your Soul* (San Francisco: HarperCollins, 2006), p. 9.

6   Ibid., p. 9.

will use that simple routine to reprioritize and renew our life together in Christ.

We assume that the servants in the parable welcomed the invited guests in a positive manner. That may not be an assumption Christians can make so easily of themselves. Thielicke suggests that many Christians may be 'poor proclaimers of all that joy.' Nietzsche had a point when he quipped, 'You will have to look more redeemed if I am to believe in your Redeemer.'[7]

The picture of the servants going out into the streets and alleys to bring in the poor, the crippled, the blind, and the lame is consistent with Jesus' advice to His host, the prominent Pharisee. The picture of expectation is consistent throughout. Only the humble fit through the narrow door, and only the humble are the true recipients of the invitation. The servants are ordered to compel the poor, the lame, and the blind to come in. But this compelling must not be misconstrued as forcing people into the banquet. Their invitation is compelling because it is so positive and inviting. As C. S. Lewis says in *Surprised by Joy*, 'The words..."compel them to come in" have been so abused by wicked people that we shudder at them; but, properly understood, they plumb the depth of the Divine mercy. The hardness of God is kinder than the softness of men, and His compulsion is our liberation.'[8]

The end of Jesus' parable is sobering. The master told his servants, 'Let me tell you, not one of those originally invited is going to get so much as a bite at my dinner party' (Luke 14:24, MSG). How's that for finishing the table fellowship on a high note! Jesus was never about making people feel good at the expense of their souls. What could the Pharisees say to

---

7   Helmut Thielicke, *The Waiting Father*, p. 187.

8   C. S. Lewis, *Surprised by Joy* (New York: Collins, 1972), p. 183.

that? I imagine that they looked blank and didn't know what to say. How did they get up from the table? Somebody must have broken the silence with some inane comment about the food or the weather, but it wasn't Jesus.

TWO STORIES

Two stories illustrate what Jesus had in mind when He told the parable of the great banquet: King David's hospitality to Mephibosheth, the crippled son of Jonathan (2 Sam. 9:1-13), and the Apostle Paul's survival meal at sea en route to Rome (Acts 27:27-38). Both situations were a matter of life and death. Mephibosheth was the lone survivor of the house of Saul and, according to the political realities of the age, the final target for David's revenge against his arch-enemy Saul. Paul was a prisoner, under guard, aboard a ship buffeted by hurricane-force winds that was in danger of sinking. In the middle of power politics and shipwreck, we have two wonderful descriptions of table fellowship.

David inquired, 'Is there anyone still left of the house of Saul to whom I can show kindness for Jonathan's sake?' (2 Sam. 9:1, NIV). Any other potentate would be thinking revenge, but David is thinking reconciliation. Love for Jonathan instead of any lingering hate for Saul led to an initiative to bless rather than curse the house of Saul. David was looking for an *enemy* to love.[9] When Mephibosheth was called before the king, he must have wondered if he was about to be sentenced to death. He bowed low before the king as a sign of respect.

David knew him by name: 'Mephibosheth!' the king announced. 'Behold, I am your servant,' Mephibosheth replied. 'Don't be afraid,' David said, echoing the first words of

---

9   Eugene H. Peterson, *Leap Over A Wall: Earthy Spirituality for Everyday Christians* (San Francisco: HarperCollins, 1998), p. 174.

the gospel (2 Sam. 9:7, ESV). 'I will show you kindness for the sake of your father Jonathan, and I will restore to you all the land of Saul your father, and you shall eat at my table always.' Mephibosheth bowed down and said, 'What is your servant, that you should show regard for a dead dog such as I?'

Mephibosheth is the perfect illustration of the kind of person Jesus invites to His banquet: physically weak, spiritually spent, living in fear, and without hope in the world. Mephibosheth is a picture of all those who respond to Christ's invitation. He was called out of fear, by a grace and love he did not earn, to sit at the king's table for life. Is there anyone like that in your life, who is broken and needy? Someone to whom you can show the kindness of God for Christ's sake?

The second story is even more unusual than the first. After fourteen days of going without food, and in the midst of a storm that threatened to break apart the ship at any moment, Paul the prisoner hosted a meal for all on board. He urged them all to eat and reiterated an incredible promise, '"Not one of you will lose a single hair from his head." After he said this, he took some bread and gave thanks to God in front of them all. Then he broke it and began to eat' (Acts 27:34-35, NIV). The language here is very similar to that used to describe the Holy Eucharist. Paul, like Jesus, took bread, gave thanks to God, and broke it, and then they began to eat. Sailors and prisoners alike were invited by the apostle of the Lord Jesus Christ to eat in the midst of a storm. It was not the Eucharist. Paul didn't use Christ's words of institution, but his actions remind us of the Lord's when He took bread and broke it and gave it to the disciples. The same verbs are in play: take, bless, break, and eat. There is a eucharistic feel to a common meal among pagans when God is thanked and His name is lifted up. In the midst of the storm, Paul broke bread and gave thanks to God, and they were all encouraged.

Mephibosheth sitting at David's table and Paul breaking bread among pagans picture the humble hospitality of God's grace. Through these stories, we can visualize the humility of God's redemptive provision overcoming the humiliation of the fallen human condition.

Jesus underscored the costly nature of this grace by following up the parable of the great banquet with His call for fully devoted disciples: 'If anyone comes to me and does not hate his own father and mother and wife and children and brothers and sisters, yes, and even his own life, he cannot be my disciple. Whoever does not bear his own cross and come after me cannot be my disciple' (Luke 14:26-27). Luke connects Jesus' table manners—'do not invite your friends, your brothers or sisters, your relatives, or your rich neighbors...[but instead] invite the poor, the crippled, the lame, the blind'—to Jesus' call to discipleship: 'let go of father, mother, spouse, children, brothers, sisters—yes, even one's own self!' (Luke 14:26 MSG).

Instead of using people for our self-interests, Jesus invites us into fellowship with Himself for the sake of redeeming the lost. The principle of the expendable life, your life for mine, is rejected, and the principle of the cross, my life for yours, is embraced. Table manners in Jesus' Kingdom ethic are as radical as they are life-fulfilling. With Christ at the head of the table, we are reminded that anyone who loses his or her life for Christ's sake finds it.

DISCUSSION:

1. Why do you think this prominent Pharisee invited Jesus to dinner? If you were to host Jesus, what would be your motive?

2. Describe the attitudes and actions that swirled around this emotionally charged table fellowship. What makes this Pharisee a cagey host?

3. How do you think Jesus' advice about the seating arrangement and the guest list was received?

4. What do you think of when you read the description of the apostle Paul in the midst of the storm urging his fellow prisoners to eat and promising them deliverance (Acts 27:27-38)? Can a meal with unsaved strangers make us think of Holy Communion?

5

Daily Bread

Give us this day our daily bread, and forgive us our
debts, as we also have forgiven our debtors... Therefore do not be anxious, saying, 'What shall we eat?'
or 'What shall we drink?' or 'What shall we wear?'
For the Gentiles seek after all these things, and your
heavenly Father knows that you need them all.

Matthew 6:11-12, 31-32

Words are important, and just the right word can make all
the difference. One carefully chosen word can express the
most profound meaning and lift up the most important
truth. The word *daily* in the fourth petition of the Lord's
Prayer is one such word. Down through the centuries,
the church has struggled over the meaning of *daily*. One
would think that the meaning of *daily bread* could not
be more obvious, but that has not always been the case.
Early church theologians assumed that this term must
have referred to something more than ordinary food. Jesus
couldn't just be talking about everyday food! He must be
referring to spiritual nourishment. Today, we have the
opposite problem. Most American Christians think daily
bread is a euphemism for material success.

The revelatory quality of a word can be abused in two
directions, downward or upward. Both ways empty the
word of its true meaning. 'Sacrilege downward takes the
form of blasphemy, language used to defile and desecrate,'

59

writes Eugene Peterson. 'Sacrilege upward takes place when language is inflated into balloons of abstraction... Pretentious language is as much a violation of the sacred core of language as blasphemy and cant.'[1] Peterson continues:

> When it comes to reading and responding to Scripture the danger of violations upward is much greater than that of violations downward for the simple reason that it is more difficult to detect. Outright blasphemy—an angry 'God dammit!'—calls more attention to itself than obsequious piety—for example, 'precious and exalted, holy and incomparable God Almighty...' intoned in a quavering voice. Ironically, the latter may be more a desecration of language than the former.[2]

The fourth petition, *Give us today our daily bread*, was vulnerable to sacrilege upward. Since the first three petitions 'express our concern for God's glory in relation to his name, rule and will,' it seemed to early interpreters that the descent from the sublime (the glory of God) to the mundane (basic human needs) was too great.[3] Yet the prayer itself was meant to be an antidote against sacrilege upward. Jesus gave the prayer as a model for how to pray and for how not to pray, like pagans with endless repetition and extensive formulas.

This immediate and intimate personal relating to 'our heavenly Father' would have impressed the Pharisees as entirely too familiar. The use of 'Abba' (Father) conveys the warmth of the Father-child relationship. 'Hallowed be your name' means 'let your name be made holy.' The Name represents who God

---

1   Eugene H. Peterson, *Eat This Book*, p. 138.

2   Ibid., p. 139.

3   John Stott, *Christian Counter-Culture: The Message of the Sermon on the Mount* (Downers Grove, Illinois: InterVarsity Press, 1978), p. 146.

is and what God has done. The Name stands for everything about God. To pray this prayer is to include ourselves in the prayer request that God's holiness would be reflected in our obedience—in the totality of our lives.

The second petition, 'let your kingdom come', encompasses everything under the sovereign rule of God, and the third petition underscores the extent of that kingdom, 'let your will be done on earth as in heaven.' All three petitions are integrally related. God's name, kingdom, and will are all bound up together. John Stott summarizes: 'What Jesus bids us pray is that life on earth may come to approximate more nearly life in heaven. For the expression "on earth as it is in heaven" seems to apply equally to the hallowing of God's name, the spreading of his kingdom and the doing of his will.'[4]

We move easily from the *you-petitions* to the *we-petitions*. In the words of Stott, 'Having expressed our burning concern for his glory, we now express our humble dependence on his grace.'[5] The focus on our Father's name, kingdom and will is consistent with His concern for our need of food, forgiveness, and deliverance from evil. But some of the early church fathers didn't quite see it that way:

> It seemed to them improper, especially after the noble three opening petitions relating to God's glory, that we should abruptly descend to so mundane and material a concern. So they allegorized the petition. The bread he meant must be spiritual, they said. Early church fathers like Tertullian, Cyprian and Augustine thought the reference was either to 'the invisible bread of the Word of God' or to the Lord's Supper.[6]

---

4   John Stott, *Christian Counter-Culture* p. 147.

5   Ibid.

6   Ibid., p. 148.

Augustine attributed three meanings to daily bread: (1) food necessary for the body; (2) the visible hallowed bread of Holy Communion; (3) the invisible bread of the Word of God. 'Jerome in the Vulgate translated the Greek word for "daily" by the monstrous adjective "supersubstantial".'[7] Thankfully, the Reformers reacted to this spiritualizing. Calvin said, 'This is exceedingly absurd.' Luther saw the bread as 'a symbol for everything necessary for the preservation of this life, like food, a healthy body, good weather, house, home, wife, children, good government and peace.'[8]

Ironically, the debate over what kind of bread we are to pray for was made more complicated by this little word, 'daily'. For years, no one could find this word in any other Greek literature. There was no reference to it in classical Greek. In the literature of the philosophers, poets, dramatists, and historians, there was no mention of *epiousion*. It was one of the five hundred or so words in the Greek New Testament that cannot be found anywhere else in Greek literature. This led to speculation about the unique character of this word. Some scholars suggested that 'the Spirit modified the secular Greek to give it a distinctive "Holy Spirit" cast, and then seeded it with freshly coined "Holy Spirit" words to confirm its exalted status as the language of revelation... This language, "biblical Greek," was exclusive to the Bible and never profaned by common use. A German theologian, Richard Rothe, went so far as to call it the "language of the Holy Ghost".'[9] Lancelot Andrewes, the leader of the King James translators, called it 'angel's food'. Origen couldn't imagine Jesus asking us to pray for a plain loaf of bread. He said it must mean, 'the bread for

---

7   John Stott, *Christian Counter-Culture* p. 148.

8   Ibid., p. 149.

9   Eugene H. Peterson, *Eat This Book*, p. 144.

which we should ask is spiritual... "the living bread that comes down from heaven".' [10]

Then, in 1897, the mystery behind many of these special words was solved by an archeological discovery in a village garbage dump at Oxyrhynchus on the Nile, 100 miles south of Cairo, Egypt. Two British archeologists, Bernard Grenfell and Arthur Hunt, unearthed scraps of paper (papyri). Written on these scraps of paper—discarded grocery lists, bills, receipts, accounts, notes, etc.—the archeologists began discovering these unliterary Greek words. 'All those special words that occurred nowhere else in written records, those "Holy Ghost" words, were all the time buried in the town garbage dump, preserved under Egyptian sand. They were all the street words, spontaneous, unstudied expressions out of the immediacy of workplace and kitchen.' [11]

Peterson tells the story well:

> Seventeen hundred years after Origen, Albert Debrunner, a professor at the University of Bern, was going over some of the Oxyrhynchus scraps of wastepaper at his library worktable and discovered the very word, *epiousion*, in an ancient housekeeping book, a shopping list that also included chickpeas and straw... And there it stands: perhaps at the very moment that Jesus was on a Galilean hillside teaching his disciples to pray for daily bread (*arton epiousion*—or their Aramaic equivalent), down in Egypt a mother was writing out a shopping list for her teenage son as she sent him off to market, emphasizing that the bread was to be fresh, today's bread—"Don't let that baker

---

10   Eugene H. Peterson, *Eat This Book*, p. 149.

11   Ibid., p. 145.

sell you any stale, day-old bread, make sure it's fresh (*epi-ousion*) bread!"[12]

There we have it: our need for bread 'stands at the heart of the Prayer. Contrary to the tendency that set in early in church history to spiritualize this request and to depreciate one's physical, material needs, Jesus' ministry demonstrated how seriously he took one's physical needs.'[13]

FOOD AND FORGIVENESS

What food is to the body, forgiveness is to the soul. By presenting these two petitions back-to-back, Jesus underscores our dependence upon God both physically and spiritually. 'Forgiveness is as indispensable to the life and health of the soul as food is for the body.'[14] We owe God our obedience, and whenever we come up short, we are in debt to him. Sin generates a debt that we cannot pay any more than we can produce bread on our own. Food and forgiveness are essential for life, and neither of them can be self-produced.

For many in America, we have all but lost this sense of dependence upon God for our food. Most of us take our abundance of food for granted. On several occasions, my Ghanaian brother David Mensah has said that he'd like to take his mother to a modern, Western supermarket just to see the look on her face. After traveling to northern Ghana and to Mongolia, this fourth petition takes on greater meaning for me. We have lost this sense of dependence upon God for basic provisions.

But our dependence is not only for food, but for forgiveness as well. People often don't sense any great need for God,

---

12 Eugene H. Peterson, *Eat This Book*, pp. 149-50.

13 Robert A. Guelich, *The Sermon on the Mount: A Foundation for Understanding* (Waco, Texas: Word Books, 1982), p. 312.

14 John Stott, *Christian Counter-Culture*, p. 149.

whether for food or forgiveness. They think that they're nice enough, so they don't need much forgiveness! A trip to the grocery store or their favorite fast-food restaurant meets the need for food, and a trip to the driving range or Nordstrom's or Starbucks or church or the office makes them feel good enough about themselves that they don't need much forgiveness.

The Lord's Prayer teaches us that if we are going to follow Jesus, we should learn to depend upon Him for all our needs. 'The supplying of one's physical, material needs, the forgiveness of sins, and the deliverance from the power of Satan were earmarks of Jesus' ministry.'[15] This is what it meant to pray 'let your kingdom come, let your will be done on earth as it is in heaven.'

FOOD FOR THE BODY

Daily bread implies a basic 'no frills' diet that supports a healthy lifestyle, but for many of us, our diet is anything but simple and basic. Are we in danger of taking food and eating too seriously? Has something gone wrong with our appetite for food? Are we lusting after food? Gourmet cooking classes, upscale dining, and the popular cable TV channel Food Network may suggest that we have a problem in this area. C. S. Lewis offers an interesting analogy: 'You can get a large audience together for a strip-tease act—that is, to watch a girl undress on the stage. Now suppose you come to a country where you could fill a theater by simply bringing a covered plate on to the stage and then slowly lifting the cover so as to let everyone see, just before the lights went out, that it contained a mutton chop or a bit of bacon, would you not think that in that country something had gone wrong with the appetite for food?'[16]

---

15   Robert A. Guelich, *The Sermon on the Mount*, p. 315.

16   C. S. Lewis, *Mere Christianity*, p. 96.

When I was young, my grandparents would take our family to an all-you-could-eat Swedish smorgasbord to celebrate special occasions. Every time we went, my brother and I ate until we could hardly move. Who could resist the chef's large slices of succulent roast beef, roasted turkey and smoked ham? You could go back as many times as you wanted. My brother liked the twelve-foot-long dessert table piled high with every kind of dessert you could imagine: pies, custards, puddings, cakes, hot fudge sundaes, brownies, and soufflés. You name it, they had it. We tried to eat our money's worth and more.

At home, we ate sensibly. My mother fixed good, nutritional meals. The smorgasbord was synonymous with over-indulgence, but we felt there was nothing wrong with that except for the bloated feeling you suffered afterwards. In those days, eating was not the major health issue that it is today. Nor were we aware of eating being an important spiritual issue. If you had accused us of gluttony, we would not have known what you were talking about. My grandparents and my parents never drank alcohol. My mother didn't even use cooking wine. Yet for some reason, my family never looked at eating the way they looked at drinking—as a spiritual issue.

The trend we see in cooking magazines and TV shows is to make a big deal about eating. We don't just serve potatoes, we serve roasted fingerling potatoes with organic rosemary buds, thyme, and European butter. It's not good enough to cook well and have it taste great. You have to search for a certain kind of vegetable or slice of beef, pay an outrageous price for it, and list every ingredient used in the sauce in the description. Then you must talk about it incessantly at the table. 'Give us today our daily bread' implies a basic food necessity. Jesus did not teach His disciples to pray, 'Give us this day our filet mignon with a superb French wine, and for dessert a choice between a crème brûlée and a chocolate lava cake.'

In the 70s, Virginia was introduced to the *More-with-Less Cookbook* published by the Mennonites. This cookbook was designed to prod over-fed North Americans to eat responsibly, to enjoy more while eating less, and to be sensitive to the world food crisis. As author Doris Janzen Longacre says, 'There is a way of wasting less, eating less, and spending less which gives not less but more.' The recipes in the cookbook were based on economy of money, time, and energy as well as food related to good health. It was a cookbook with a thesis: 'There is a way which gives not less but more. More joy, more peace, less guilt; more physical stamina, less overweight and obesity; more to share and less to hoard for ourselves.' Longacre's basic idea is hard to refute: 'We have gotten less with more. Paul's words to Timothy, "If we have food and clothing, with these we shall be content," have no meaning for us.'[17] Her thesis reminds us of the wisdom of Proverbs: 'Two things I ask of you; …Remove far from me falsehood and lying; give me neither poverty nor riches, feed me with the food that is needful for me, lest I be full and deny you and say, "Who is the Lord?" or lest I be poor and steal and profane the name of my God' (Prov. 30:7-9).

There is a right way and a wrong way to be serious about food. Eating is serious, but in a well-defined way. C. S. Lewis encourages us to think about food '*theologically*, as the vehicle of the Blessed Sacrament; *ethically* in view of our duty to feed the hungry; *socially*, because the table is from time immemorial the place for talk; *medically*, as all dyspeptics know. Yet we do not bring bluebooks (prayer

---

17   Doris Janzen Longacre, *More-with-Less Cookbook* (Scottdale, Pennsylvania: Herald Press, 1976), p. 20.

books) to dinner nor behave there as if we were in church. And it is gourmets, not saints, who come nearest to doing so. Animals are always serious about food.'[18]

On this issue we are more like the typical pagan than we would like to admit. We succumb to the temptation of taking that which has appropriate place and value and exaggerating its importance. Greed and coveting does this with possessions. Lust does it with sex, and overindulgence or gluttony does it with food. Writing on the seven deadly sins, Henry Fairlie observes, 'We have become absurdly interested in our food. We think, read, worry, talk about it. We expect it to be too foolproof a nourishment— of our spirits as well as our bodies—to enchant us too continuously. Our attitude to it is also idolatrous. We have made our food a golden calf. "We are what we eat," we used to say glibly, but now we seem to believe it.'[19]

Of course, one doesn't have to be fat to have an idolatrous relationship with food. A person may talk more about dieting than they do about food, but it is the same basic idolatry. Someone may look like they spent the last six months in a concentration camp, emaciated to the point of starvation, but suffer the same obsession as the obese. 'This obsession with one's food is a reflection of an obsession with our bodies.'[20]

What is the antidote for this obsessive self-love, this obsession with our bodies and our food? The solution lies in another appetite—in another hunger. To eat without fixation and fuss requires a focus not on ourselves, but on the Lord.

---

18 C. S. Lewis, *The Four Loves* (New York: Harcourt Brace & Company, 1960), p. 98.

19 Henry Fairlie, *The Seven Deadly Sins Today* (University of Notre Dame Press, 1979), p. 159.

20 Ibid., p. 164.

This may sound pious, but it is true. Those who hunger and thirst after righteousness are filled, but those who hunger for a sensual experience, whether of food or drink or sex or thinness, are left empty—always. This hunger and thirst for righteousness relates back to Psalm 23. The Lord prepares a table before us in the presence of our enemies, even when the enemy is obesity or bulimia or anorexia.

FOOD FOR THE SOUL

When Moses was leading the Israelites through the desert, Yahweh put them on a manna diet. The *first* message to be found in manna was that there was more to life than being well fed and physically satisfied. It didn't take long for the Israelites to compare their existence in the wilderness to their fond, but distorted, remembrance of life back in Egypt. 'If only we had died by the Lord's hand in Egypt! There we sat round pots of meat and ate all the food we wanted, but you have brought us out into this desert to starve this entire assembly to death' (Exod. 16:3, NIV).

Immediate material gratification is a strong temptation when compared with the demands of long-term spiritual growth. It is hard for some people to grasp the relationship between living and meaning. If we allow it, foster it, or give in to it, there can be a huge gap between daily living and eternal significance. One-dimensional existence misses the meaning of life. The great truths of God and salvation are ignored. When we reduce life to appearances and appetites, there is no vision for anything other than that which is literal, physical, and material. Our dog, Maggie, lives this kind of one-dimensional life. She's fed twice a day, morning and evening. *Science Diet* dog food plus a little exercise and affection make for a happy dog. We humans are in danger of copying a dog's existence when we say to ourselves, 'You have ample goods laid up for many years; relax, eat, drink, be merry' (Luke 12:19).

Satisfying our physical appetites at the expense of our soul is a major issue in the Bible. It is fine to care about our physical well-being, but we must care first and foremost about our relationship with the Lord. We need to eat and exercise, but there is more to living than following our physical and material appetites. This was the issue that confronted Jesus in the wilderness. 'After fasting forty days and nights, he was hungry. And the tempter came and said to him, "If you are the Son of God, command these stones to become loaves of bread." Jesus answered, 'It is written: "Man shall not live by bread alone, but by every word that comes from the mouth of God"' (Matt. 4:2-4). With these words, Jesus pointed back to the meaning of manna. He emphasized the priority of life in the Spirit over physical life alone.

To the Israelites, their Egyptian oppressors epitomized the good life. They had forgotten why God called Moses to deliver them: 'I have surely seen the affliction of my people who are in Egypt and have heard their cry... I know their sufferings, and I have come down to deliver them' (Exod. 3:7-8). The Israelites envied their oppressors and the very lifestyle that had made them poor. In the wilderness, all they could remember was the all-you-could-eat Egyptian buffet. Looking back at their old way of life, they seem to have forgotten the slavery and the misery.

Like the Israelites, we are often tempted to live only on the surface. When life is shrunk down to the tangible, visceral, physical, and material world, it seems a whole lot easier to cope with than the journey of faith in a real-world wilderness. The sad truth is that the Israelites began to talk as if they preferred humiliation under oppressive masters to humility before their merciful God.

The reason God allowed Israel to experience hunger in the wilderness was so that Israel would learn to turn to God. But instead of praying to God for His provision, they murmured and complained and wished they were back in their old lifestyle. God responded to their need, in spite of their grumbling. They called it manna; God called it bread from heaven.

The Israelites questioned, 'What is it?' but God's *second* message from manna was also clear. Manna was not only food for the body, but food for the soul. From the start, manna's purpose went beyond physical nourishment. God's physical provision was meant to be a reminder of His people's spiritual dependence. God put the Israelites on a healthy spiritual and physical diet. The Lord had no desire to compete with Egyptian cuisine. He fed them; he didn't spoil them. What a good diet can do for our bodies, manna did for the sojourners in the wilderness.

Many of us try to eat healthy and exercise often. We are convinced that diet is a key factor in staying in shape and feeling healthy. But the same concern that we have for proper physical nourishment often has not carried over into a hunger for proper spiritual nourishment. We alternate between starving ourselves spiritually and eating a lot of spiritual junk food. A diet rich in Christian romances and end-times fiction is like living on Big Macs and fries. They may taste good, but they're not that good for us. It is sad when so-called Christian publishers feed people's fantasies rather than their faith.

Most of us would be doing well if we meditated on God's Word the way we focus on food. I know that I have been saying that the physical and spiritual aspects of table fellowship work in tandem: The biblical writers wanted us to link these two concerns together. That is why eating becomes a metaphor for studying God's revelation in the Bible. Since we are pretty good at eating to maintain our physical well-being, we should be just as interested in studying God's Word to maintain our spiritual health. As the psalmist said, 'How sweet are your words to my taste, sweeter than honey to my mouth!' (Ps. 119:103). The wilderness diet of manna and quail was designed by God to humble the people and focus their attention on Him, their Creator and Lord. Just as an athlete's performance is related to diet and discipline, the depth of the Israelites' worship was related to diet and devotion. The timing of God's provision emphasized daily dependence and Sabbath rest. When considering 'food for the soul,' these are two important issues. Daily dependence upon God, and participating in Sabbath rest and worship, are both designed to set the rhythm for the week.

The nature of God's provision of manna to the Israelites also underscores our need to seek God *daily*. It may be important for us to ask ourselves some pointed questions: If we have lost interest in worship or in fellowship with God's people, is it because we lack daily fellowship with God? Are we confused over God's will as it relates to work, finances and family because we don't study God's Word? Do we complain that Christians have let us down, when in fact we have let ourselves down spiritually by refusing to practice even a very basic spiritual discipline, such as daily prayer and Bible reading? In a preface to one of his devotional books, Andrew Murray wrote: 'Meditate on this thought: The feeble state of my spiritual life is mainly due to the lack of time day by day in fellowship with God. New life will dawn in many a soul as a result of time spent in prayer alone with God.'[21] I hope these questions don't

---

21   Andrew Murray, *God's Best Secrets* (Grand Rapids, MI: Kregel, 1993), p. 9

come across legalistically. There is no simple formula for true spiritual growth, but there are practical ways that we can embrace God's presence and enjoy the fellowship of believers.

FOOD FOR THE HUNGRY

Jesus told us to pray for **our** daily bread. This is not an individual prayer for one's own food but a corporate prayer for each other's food. If the Lord gives me my daily food, do I have a responsibility to see that others get their daily food? Are we in this experience of living and eating together or alone? For the followers of Jesus, the answer seems pretty obvious. Jesus makes caring for the poor and needy personal. 'Truly, I say to you, as you did it to one of the least of these my brothers and sisters, you did it to me' (Matt. 25:40).

After college, I spent eight months in Chung Li, Taiwan, teaching at a science and engineering college. I lived in a dorm with other rookie teachers and ate with the students in little food shops around the campus. The change in diet and several severe bouts of food poisoning resulted in a weight loss of thirty pounds. Up until then, the lack of food had never been an issue in my life. Good food was always readily available. But now I began to think about where my next meal was coming from and whether my body could handle it. What I had taken for granted all my life became a real prayer concern. The answer to my prayer came in the form of a frail, eighty-four-year-old Southern Baptist missionary who had taught her cook from northern China to prepare great American-style meals. A caring, Chinese Christian brother encouraged her to invite me for lunch, and she did. Every day at noon, the two of us, with some sixty years between us, enjoyed good food and conversation. In this context, I was very grateful for my *daily bread*.

There is plenty of admonition in the Bible about feeding the hungry: The Lord expects us to 'share [our] bread with the hungry' and 'pour [ourselves] out for the hungry' (Isa. 58:7, 10). One of the strongest ministries of our church in San Diego is called 'The Ladle Ministry.' For over forty years, the church has fed the poor on Sunday afternoons. Two to three hundred people enjoy a hot meal prepared and served by members of the church. Through this ministry, a number of people over time have moved from the dining room to the sanctuary and have joined us for worship. For some, being served in our church dining room has been the first step on the road of transformation in Christ.

Sometimes feeding the poor happens on a large scale, as just described. Other times, it involves reaching out to an individual in need. I joke that I met David Mensah, one of my dearest friends, over corn. In the early eighties, I was a teacher at Ontario Bible College. One day, I heard a rumor that a new student from Ghana was afraid to come out of his room. I decided to check it out. I knocked on the student's dormitory door and met for the first time a brother in Christ whom I would grow to deeply love and respect. The immensity of this man's identity, however, was concealed by the shy demeanor of a half-starved African boy who looked like a bewildered refugee locked up in prison. He was in a state of total culture shock. He had not eaten for several days. David had tried the cafeteria food once and had gotten so sick that he had not left his room again. I did not know what to do to help this boy. Thankfully, my wife Virginia is quicker than me. When I told her about David, she said, 'Bring him home!' I will let David tell the rest in his own words:

That night, Virginia cooked corn, along with some North American dishes, for their supper. I didn't even look at the other things but ate that boiled corn like a pig. I ate and ate and ate. Doug and Virginia could only watch in amazement. But, preoccupied as I was, I did notice the expressions of joy on their faces. At last this young man from Africa was able to take nourishment. The food settled comfortably into my stomach. The professor informed the cafeteria manager of what had happened and from that day on, corn was always available at the cafeteria.[22]

For the last twenty years, David and his wife Brenda have led a ministry team in northern Ghana that feeds the poor, cares for widows, and plants the gospel. Literally thousands in the northern region have benefited from their holistic ministry, which includes food cooperatives, agricultural expertise, a fish hatchery, animal husbandry, and church planting. The Ghana Rural Integrated Development (GRID) ministry team preaches Christ in ten thousand ways—offering our daily bread is one important way.[23]

Health and holiness are inseparable. Good eating habits and feeding on the Word of God are dynamically integrated in the Christian's life. We need discipline and wisdom in what we feed our bodies and in what we feed our souls. Gratitude for our daily food is expressed in the same breath that we thank the Lord for our salvation through the cross of Christ.

Discussion:

1. What do you make of these two petitions in the Lord's Prayer, one for daily bread, the other for daily

---

22 David Mensah, *Kwabena: An African Boy's Journey of Faith* (Belleville, Ontario, Canada: Essence Publishing, 1998), p. 213.

23 To learn more about this important gospel ministry in northern Ghana, go to www.GRID-NEA.org.

forgiveness? How do you see the relationship between food and forgiveness?

2. God put the Israelites on a spiritual diet and weaned them off their all-you-can-eat Egyptian buffet. What lessons can we learn from God's miraculous provision of bread from heaven? How do these lessons apply to our physical and spiritual needs?

3. Jesus said, 'Blessed are those who hunger and thirst for righteousness, for they will be filled' (Matt. 5:6, NIV). How are our true appetites satisfied?

4. Would many of our food issues be resolved if we changed our spiritual diet?

6

Real Food

For my flesh is true food and my blood is true drink.
Whoever feeds on my flesh and drinks my blood
abides in me, and I in him.

John 6:55-56

Hunger—the literal, physical, need for food—is a pointer to an even greater need, a deeper hunger. Everything we have been saying in *Table Grace* points to more than mere hospitality—more than food—more than socializing. There is more to the 'table in the presence of our enemies' than material provision—much more. The working lunch between Abraham and the triune God was not about food, but about the Promise. Jesus used dinner at the prominent Pharisee's home to shake up the religious and social conventions of the day and to invite the outcasts to be insiders in the Kingdom of God. Jesus used our 'everyday, ordinary life—our sleeping, eating, going-to-work, and walking-around life' to show us what is truly important in life (Rom. 12:1, MSG).

Satisfying our physical appetites at the expense of our soul is a major issue in the Bible. It is fine to care about our physical well-being, but we ought to care first and foremost about our relationship with the Lord. Following his

forty days of fasting in the wilderness, Jesus was confronted by the tempter, who said, 'If you are the Son of God, tell
these stones to become bread.' Jesus answered, 'It is written: "People do not live on bread alone, but on every word
that comes from the mouth of God"' (Matt. 4:3-4, NIV).
Food is necessary. No doubt about it. But there is something far more important than food, and Jesus used His
own famished condition to prove it.

While Jesus talked with the Samaritan woman at
Jacob's well, His disciples went into town in search of food.
When they returned, they urged him to eat: 'Rabbi, eat!'
But Jesus responded, 'I have food to eat that you do not
know about.' The disciples still didn't get it. They thought
somebody must have brought him some food (Sometimes
the disciples could be so literal!). 'My food,' said Jesus, 'is to
do the will of him who sent me and to accomplish his work'
(John 4:31-34).

When Jesus played the role of host to the giant crowd,
He not only met their physical need for a meal, He also
used food and drink as a symbol of a far greater need. He
insisted on a truth too deep for humanistic consumption
and everyone, including His closest disciples, struggled
with what He meant.

NARRATIVE ART

John Pryor has called the sixth chapter of the Gospel of
John 'a masterpiece of John's narrative art.'[1] John combines
sign, dialogue, and *discourse* into 'one essential message:
that Jesus is the Bread of Life, the source of divine nourishment for humanity.'[2] Our physical need for food is no more

---

1   John W. Pryor, *John: Evangelist of the Covenant People* (Downers Grove,
     Illinois: InterVarsity Press, 1992), p. 29.

2   Ibid.

real and no less literal than our need for the Incarnate Son of God. Daily bread and Bread from Heaven share the same reality. Both are a human necessity. We can't live without food and we can't live without Jesus.

This episode in the Gospel of John is a unified progression that builds to a climax—a pivotal turning point in the Gospel that shapes the story of Jesus. The episode is made up of two nature miracles—Jesus feeding the multitude and Jesus walking on the sea—followed by a dialogue with the crowd that ends in debate and confusion, as well as a discourse with the disciples that ends in denial. There are three miracles in all, and the third is the most difficult to believe. The third miracle is the message of the gospel. Jesus said, 'I am the bread of life... If anyone eats of this bread, he will live forever. And the bread that I will give for the life of the world is my flesh' (John 6:48, 51). At the end, the great crowd have left on their own accord. Instead of being sent away by the disciples to get food (Mark 6:36), they have sent themselves away because they can't stomach Jesus' teaching.

From the start, John embeds hints of significance in the narrative, informing us that 'the Passover, the feast of the Jews, was at hand.' He reports moments of suspense ('Jesus, knowing that they intended to come and make him king by force, withdrew again to a mountain by himself'). At times, the significance and the suspense coincide, as when Jesus surprises the disciples on the rough sea and says, '*I am*, be not afraid!'

The passion of a passage is found in the tension in the text, and there is plenty of tension here. There is tension between physical needs and spiritual needs, between food for the stomach and food for the soul, and between popular, political, messianic expectations and the way of redemption graciously provided by God. There is tension between 'accessibility' and 'abstraction', between literal bread and metaphoric bread. There is tension between the popular Jesus, the Jesus people thought they knew ('Is this not Jesus, the son of Joseph, whose father and mother we know?') and the real Jesus ('the bread that comes down from heaven and gives life to the world'). There is tension between the disciples who reject the Bread of Life and the Twelve who seem to be left with no other choice than to follow the Holy One of God. From this whole episode in the life of Christ we learn that if we are going to follow Jesus, there is only one Jesus to follow, the one who is the Way, the Truth, and the Life (John 14:6).

THE QUESTION

The Jewish Passover Festival was near, and the disciples must have thought that everything was coming together. Success was just around the corner. The miraculous healings alone catapulted Jesus into celebrity status. But Jesus had other ideas. Instead of capitalizing on the momentum, he focused on two inseparable concerns: daily bread and the bread of life.

Looking out over the approaching massive crowd, Jesus asked Philip, 'Where shall we *buy* bread for these people to eat?' The question undoubtedly took Philip by surprise, because up to this point feeding the multitude was not his problem—not anybody's problem in particular. But the question posed by Jesus implied responsibility and obligation. Unexpectedly, a huge burden was suddenly thrust upon Philip.

Confronted, but probably not convicted, by this overwhelming demand, Philip immediately thought in terms of budget. He could hardly be blamed because his first thought was about money. Jesus, after all, had asked him where they could *buy* bread. Nor could Philip be blamed for thinking how much it would cost to give each person a bite! He had the good sense to know that the very least they could do was beyond what they could afford.

If Jesus had asked His question in a more spiritual way, maybe Philip would have responded more piously. If Jesus had said, 'Philip, do you believe God can feed this crowd?' I am sure Philip would have said 'yes.' What else could he say? But Jesus asked a practical, logistical, monetary, supply-side question on behalf of these particular people: 'Where shall we buy bread for these people to eat?'

Jesus begins the episode with a question. We are told by John that Jesus asked this question only to test Philip. Jesus already had in mind what He would do. In fact, Jesus may have had a specific biblical text in mind when he asked Philip this question. The paradox of *buying* food and drink *without money* is precisely what the prophet Isaiah had in mind when he delivered the Lord's invitation:

> Come, everyone who thirsts, come to the waters; and he who has no money, come, buy and eat! Come, buy wine and milk without money and without price. Why do you spend your money for that which is not bread, and your labor for that which does not satisfy? Listen diligently to me, and eat what is good, and delight yourselves in rich food. (Isa. 55:1-2)

Instead of buying bread with money, the prophet envisioned buying 'food' with listening. 'Listen, listen to me, and eat what is good, and you will delight in the richest of fare.' Philip was confronted with something even greater than a colossal human need. He was faced with the opportunity of placing his faith in the Messiah to meet this apparently overwhelming need. Jesus' question was an invitation to go beyond conventional thinking and to look at meeting needs from a radically different perspective.

SHOWING COMPASSION

Giving people simply what they want may satisfy certain felt needs but make it more difficult to give them what they truly need. Obviously, there is a difference between a felt need for food and a felt need for entertainment. Meeting a basic human need is inspired by God and motivated out of compassion. Meeting a culturally induced felt need caters to selfishness and is motivated out of competition.

Pastor Leith Anderson, of Wooddale Church, near Minneapolis, sees 'the rise of consumerism' as the greatest factor impacting the church today. 'What goes for cars, doctors, tires, and schools also goes for churches. Americans go where they think they can get the best deal, or where they think their needs will be met, regardless of previous affiliations. This means that a few weeks of poor sermons, weak music, or a dirty nursery may prompt present members to start looking elsewhere.'[3] People are looking for more bang for their buck. 'More and more Americans are opting for "full service churches" that can offer quality and variety in music, extensive youth programs, diverse educational opportunities, a counseling staff, support groups, singles' ministry, athletic activities, multiple Sunday morning services, a modern nursery, and the other services and programs only available in larger churches.'[4] Today's theory is that churches need to keep up with the latest trends in music, communications,

---

3   Leith Anderson, *Dying For Change* (Minneapolis, Minnesota: Bethany House, 1990), p. 49.

4   Ibid., p. 51.

technology, architecture, and leadership if they expect to compete effectively in today's marketplace. In our rapidly changing world, churches that don't keep up will be left behind.

Under the guise of being practical, we are becoming secular. We are promoting the gospel as a product. We are trying to create brand loyalty in a highly competitive market. Andy Stanley of North Point Ministries in Atlanta writes, 'You have to identify for [your target audience] what you are selling. Are you trying to get people to buy into your church? Or are you trying to get them to buy into an environment that is relevant? Which one do you think is an easier sell?' Stanley argues that people are not looking for a generic church, just like they're not looking for a generic car. They are looking for something specific, like a sports car or an SUV or a Saab convertible. Likewise, people are 'looking for something that is relevant to their marriage, their family, their personal lives. What they are looking for is something that works for them as individuals. And that is something specific, not general.'[5]

We do not have to compete for people's attention, but we do have to be sensitive to their needs. There's a difference between compassion and competition, and discerning that difference is an act of love. John Stott warns, 'Unless we listen attentively to the voices of secular society, unless we struggle to understand them, unless we feel with modern men and women in their frustration, their alienation, their pain and even sometimes, their despair, I think that we shall lack authenticity as the followers of Jesus of Nazareth.'[6]

---

5   Andy Stanley, Lane Jones, Reggie Joiner, *7 Practices of Effective Ministry* (New York: Doubleday, 2004), p. 108.

6   John Stott, 'Secular Challenges and the Contemporary Church,' *Crux* (Regent College, September 1991), p. 2.

We can learn two things from Philip's response. First, he was challenged to meet the people's felt need for food. Jesus designated this basic human need as something significant enough to engage His disciples' attention and energy. If the people of God truly believe that men and women are physical and spiritual beings, made in the image of God, then there will be genuine concern for their physical and emotional welfare as well as their spiritual wholeness. Salvation encompasses the whole person.

The physical and spiritual dimensions of human nature are inseparable. As John Stott says, 'Our neighbor is neither a bodyless soul that we should love only his soul, nor a soulless body that we should care for its welfare alone, nor even a body-soul isolated from society. God created man, who is my neighbor, a body-soul-in-community.'[7] Jesus acknowledged the validity of meeting this physical need independently of any other consideration.

Second, Philip learned that food is a powerful analogy for our profound need for spiritual nourishment. Satisfying physical needs can be an important bridge for meeting our most fundamental need for God. In John 6, daily bread is used as a visual aid to underscore the importance of spiritual nourishment. Jesus Himself, the one, true and only source—the Bread of Life—delivers the message. As we shall see, the value of meeting this physical need and its significance in facilitating awareness of spiritual needs was not based on numbers. The success of this redemptive analogy is its appropriateness to the human person rather than its popular appeal.

The apostle Paul warned against giving people what they want instead of what they need. 'The time is com-

---

7   John Stott, *Christian Mission in the Modern World* (Downers Grove, Illinois: InterVarsity Press, 1975), pp. 29-30.

ing,' he told Timothy, 'when people will not endure sound teaching, but having itching ears they will accumulate for themselves teachers to suit their own passions, and will turn away from listening to the truth and wander off into myths' (2 Tim. 4:3-4). Evangelicals read this warning and feel that it does not pertain to them because they adhere to 'sound doctrine,' but as Kenneth Myers reminds us, 'Idols and myths can take the form of moods and sensibilities as well as stone and creed, and there are many disturbing signs that many contemporary Christians have made the limited and limiting sensibility of popular culture their own.'[8] We have become susceptible to the idolatrous moods of novelty, sentimentality, and subjectivism. Churches now compete, not only among themselves, but also with the popular culture, in a mood-producing quest for warmth and excitement. For Leith Anderson, 'Leadership in the competitive hardware industry is not too much different from leadership in the competitive church world.'[9]

In a consumer-oriented environment, it costs money to compete. The first concern for ministry is, invariably, how much it will cost. Can we afford it? Money and ministry are inextricably linked in the competitive church. Ministry is either limited or accelerated depending on how much money the church has. Without money, it appears, our hands are tied, and our great visions impossible. Think of it! God's great work of salvation is at the mercy of the economy. Perhaps part of the lesson Jesus had in store for Philip and us was that God's work is not threatened by the economy. In fact, the power of Christlike compassion is

---

8   Kenneth A. Myers, *All God's Children and Blue Suede Shoes: Christians and Popular Culture* (Wheaton, Illinois: Crossway Books, 1989), p. 87.

9   Leith Anderson, *Leadership That Works* (Minneapolis: Bethany House, 1999), p. 108.

recession-proof. It cannot be hindered by depression, inflation, unemployment, or a Wall Street downturn. Former pastor of Washington D.C.'s Fourth Presbyterian Church and U.S. Senate chaplain, Richard C. Halverson, asked, 'Is it conceivable that God's plan for world mission is at the mercy of the economy? Is it possible that the God who spoke the universe into existence, who owns the land, the silver and the gold, the cattle on a thousand hills, the earth and all its fullness, could be the victim of the economy?'[10]

Jesus is not suggesting to Philip that money has no place in the economy of ministry. Throughout the Gospels, Jesus has much to say about sacrificial giving and the spiritual discipline of stewardship. Here, however, His questioning of Philip not only serves to define legitimate need and Philip's obligation to meet that need, independent of limited financial resources, but also refocuses Philip on God's work. Ministry is not just a human endeavor, pursued by human means alone, but a spiritual endeavor, pursued in partnership with God, even when its goal is meeting physical needs.

Right from the start, Jesus distinguished between human-dependent need-meeting and God-dependent need-meeting. In themselves, the disciples had no solution for meeting this overwhelming need. In ourselves, we have no solution to the tremendous needs that people have. Only in Jesus do we find the way, the truth, and the life. Unless we are aware of that distinction, we will end up distracting ourselves from the mission God has called us to fulfill.

In this case, two disciples, Philip and Andrew, respond to this particular need for food differently. Leon Morris

---

10   Richard C. Halverson, 'Counting the Cost of a Church Rich in Resources,' *Christianity Today* (July 17, 1981), p. 42.

notes that 'Philip does not point to a solution, but to an impossibility.'[11] At least Andrew offers a possibility. Once again, Andrew is introduced as Simon Peter's brother, and once again, he is bringing someone to Jesus. The person he brings is just a little boy with cheap bread and two small fish. I wish I knew Andrew's tone of voice and facial expression when he volunteered the young boy's five small barley loaves and two small fish. Maybe he gave away his skeptical attitude when he said, 'but what are they for so many?' Or maybe he was embarrassed but hopeful that Jesus could bring something out of nothing.

HOSTING THE CROWD

Jesus plays the role of host to a massive crowd out in the countryside. The first thing he does is bring order. 'Have the people sit down.' Mark adds the detail that Jesus had them sit down in groups of a hundred or less. Then, Jesus 'took the loaves, and when he had given thanks, he distributed them to those who were seated... as much as they wanted.' A sacramental sense is conveyed even in the most basic human need-meeting. The act is solemn, holy, and administered with prayer. Craig Blomberg observes:

> What is regularly overlooked in this account is that the multitude will have almost certainly come from a wide cross-section of Galilean society. Just as a sizeable majority eked out a marginal existence, so too the simple farmers, fishermen, and homemakers of the province would have made up the largest portion of this crowd. Thus, by Pharisaic standards, one must describe this gathering as ritually impure. The desert location, moreover, implies that there is no possibility of being selective with the

---

11   Leon Morris, *The Gospel According to John* (Grand Rapids: Eerdmans, 1971), p. 343.

guest list, that some deemed as undesirables are present, and that there can be no seating plan and certainly no facility for handwashing or other cleansing rites. Pharisaic purists would have objected on multiple counts.[12]

Jesus was completely unconcerned about the very things that would have been uppermost in the minds of the Pharisees. He makes no distinction between clean and unclean. No effort is made to tithe or carry out ceremonial cleansing. The multitude is a picture of the Israelites in the wilderness. Even their orderly grouping is reminiscent of an Exodus administration that turned a crowd into a people. John tells us pointedly that the surplus of twelve baskets of barley loaves came from the little boy's five barley loaves. There was no doubt in his mind that a miracle on the order of bread from heaven had happened on the far side of the Sea of Galilee.

Ducking the Performance Trap

Meeting people's needs can prove difficult. Defining people's real needs is only half the battle. Even when genuine human needs are met, delivering people from false expectations and dependencies is an ongoing, necessary work. On full stomachs, the people were ready to make Jesus king 'by force' (John 6:15), so He withdrew into the hills by Himself. The people were longing for a political messiah who would provide peace and prosperity, and Jesus fit the bill. He performed to their expectations and then some. Who wouldn't want a miracle-working problem-solver on the throne of one's own making?

The work of meeting people's needs can become a performance trap. Under the pressure of a pleased constituency, the best intentions for Christian service may

---

12   Craig L. Blomberg, *Contagious Holiness: Jesus' Meals with Sinners* (Downers Grove, Illinois: InterVarsity Press, 2005), p. 106.

be distorted into the creation of a personality cult. In this situation, Jesus showed us how to walk out of the performance trap by insisting on the truth. The need for food was significant, but not singular. If Jesus had met only this basic need, he would have been guilty of kingdom negligence and spiritual malpractice. He called the miraculous feeding a 'sign', or a pointer, and confronted the crowds with the fact that their interest in Him was only because their stomachs were full. He persisted in using their felt need as a 'bridge' to a greater truth (John 6:27).

WALKING ON THE SEA

The second miracle in this episode was meant for the disciples only. The disciples embarked in their boat across the Sea of Tiberias without Jesus. They had rowed about three miles. It was dark and the wind was blowing strong. The sea was rough. And then they spotted Jesus coming toward them walking on the water. Understandably, these sea-hardy disciples were frightened. John says nothing about Peter getting out of the boat and trying to walk to Jesus. His emphasis is on Jesus' actions and His words: 'I am; don't be afraid.' For John, the words 'I am' are filled with the most profound meaning. They are his shorthand notation for the Incarnate Son of God. This is the first in a series of 'I am' sayings that develop Jesus' role in revelation and salvation ('I am the bread of life'—6:35, 41, 48, 51; 'I am the light of the world'—8:12; 'I am he', 8:24, 28; 'before Abraham was born, I am!'—8:58; 'I am the gate for the sheep'—10:7, 9; 'I am the good shepherd'—10:11, 14; 'I am the resurrection and the life'—11:25; 'I am who I am'—13:19; 'I am the way and the truth and the life'—14:6; 'I am the true vine'—15:1, 5).

Only after Jesus speaks are the disciples willing to take him into the boat. They are exposed to an extraordinary display of Jesus' power over nature, and they have a unique advantage over the remnant of the crowd that was left behind. Instead of unanswered questions and confusion, they know how Jesus gets across the Tiberias. Although they can't explain how He did it, the disciples see Jesus walking on the water. They are privileged to witness the second miracle. Yet the more they see of Jesus, the more they realize that they can't explain Jesus.

Proclaiming the Truth

Jesus provoked the minds and penetrated the hearts of a reluctant and distracted audience, not through a performance but through proclamation of the Word of God. Jesus accused the crowd of following Him, not because they saw the sign, but because they 'ate the loaves' and had their fill. The majority of the people seem to have been either disinterested or confused by Jesus' Bread of Life discourse. There is no hint that they expected Jesus to do anything more than meet their immediate felt need. Judging from the negative feedback Jesus received, His insistence on proclaiming the truth about Himself and salvation proved to be an ineffective marketing strategy. The people were unable or unwilling to make the transition from a physical, tangible provision to a spiritual, abstract subject.

The surest way to kill a performance is to demand something from the audience that they're unprepared to give. Jesus' proclamation required serious reflection. This was necessary if the people were interested in understanding what He had to say. But then, as now, serious reflection was not popular. Although Jesus used simple words, His complex, abstract thought required careful reflection from His hearers. He used a simple, graphic, visual aid, devoid of religious jargon, and then proceeded to develop the 'true bread from heaven' message in a radically thought-provoking way.

Abstract is a usually a pejorative term. To say that something is *abstract* is to say that it is uninteresting, impractical, and theoretical. The problem today, however, is that all serious conceptual thinking faces the danger of being dismissed as *abstract*. Unless meaning is immediately accessible, even to the casual hearer, the message is dismissed.

The connection between ancient manna and the miraculous feeding of the multitude was not lost on the crowd. In fact, they brought it up. They asked Jesus, 'Then what sign do you do, that we may see and believe you? What work do you perform?' They quoted from Exodus: 'Our fathers ate the manna in the wilderness; as it is written, "He gave them bread from heaven to eat"' (John 6:31). The crowd drew the connection between a sign from heaven and manna in the wilderness, and Jesus made the most of the connection. He declared, '"Truly, truly, I say to you, it was not Moses who gave you the bread from heaven, but my Father gives you the true bread from heaven. For the bread of God is he who comes down from heaven and gives life to the world." They said to him, "Sir, give us this bread always"' (John 6:32-34).

'Sir,' they said, 'give us this bread always.' Then Jesus declared, 'I am the bread of life; whoever comes to me shall not hunger, and whoever believes in me shall never thirst... For I have come down from heaven, not to do my own will but the will of him who sent me... For this is the will of my Father, that everyone who looks on the Son and believes in him should have eternal life, and I will raise him up on the last day.' In language reminiscent of the Israelites in the wilderness, we read, 'So the Jews grumbled about him, because he said, "I am the bread that came down from heaven."' They said, 'Is not this Jesus, the son of Joseph, whose father and mother we know? How does he now say, "I have come down from heaven"?' (John 6:35-42).

'Do not grumble among yourselves,' Jesus answered. 'No one can come to me unless the Father who sent me draws him. And I will raise him up on the last day... I am the bread of life. Your fathers ate the manna in the wilderness, and they died. This is the bread that comes down from heaven, so that one may eat of it and not die. I am the living bread that came down from heaven. If anyone eats of this bread, he will live forever. And the bread that I will give for the life of the world is my flesh' (John 6:43-51).

As a biblical object lesson, manna symbolizes God's complete provision. From the temporal to the eternal, God's provision is complete. The gift of manna covers the range of God's blessing, from the Israelites' daily bread in the wilderness to the gift of salvation through our crucified and risen Lord. Every time we break bread together, we remember that it is God who strengthens our bodies and souls. There is an inseparable connection between the manna in the wilderness, our daily bread, and the bread of the Eucharist. When the Lord gave the Israelites manna and insisted that they keep a portion of it in the Ark of the Covenant as a testimony (Exod. 16:33; Heb. 9:4), He created a biblical image that pointed forward to the Bread of Life. Jesus summed it up this way: 'This is the bread that came down from heaven, not as the bread the fathers ate and died. Whoever feeds on this bread will live forever' (John 6:58). Therefore, whenever we 'eat this bread and drink the cup, [we] proclaim the Lord's death until he comes' (1 Cor. 11:26). We remember Christ's broken body, His sacrifice for our sin and His provision for our eternal salvation. God's provision is complete in Christ and meets all of our needs body, mind and soul. 'For the bread of God is he who comes down from heaven and gives life to the world' (John 6:33).

IMPOSSIBLE TEACHING

Are we willing to communicate the gospel of Christ the way Jesus did? The transition from eating bread to eating the bread of life required a miracle. Jesus depended on the power of God to convince and convict His listeners (John 6:37, 44, 65). The Son's reliance on the Father recognizes the difficulty people have in moving from immediate felt needs to their true spiritual need. Jesus never entertained the notion that a 'command performance' was sufficient to move the people from popular opinion ('Who does he think he is? We know his parents!') to a solid confession that he is the Bread of Heaven, giving life to the world. Jesus purposed to press the truth well beyond traditional religious ideas and popular appeal.

Instead of weakening His approach under the pressure of rejection He grew more explicit, as if to clarify where His listeners stood. He insisted on elaborating powerful metaphors to the breaking point of listener credulity. His transformation of felt needs went further than even many of His disciples could accept. Jesus deliberately shocked and challenged. He actually forced His listeners to decide either for or against Him by the power of His words and the intensity of His analogies.

Without clarifying definitions and careful explanations, Jesus focused the Bread of Life and Passover lamb metaphors upon Himself. The seriousness of the cross hung over everything Jesus said. Some were angry, others were offended; nobody found the message easy. Jesus had managed to alienate just about everybody. The sobering truth in this extended discourse is that the gospel is radical communication, unsuited for neatly laid out, worldly categories and self-help comfort zones. Jesus plunged his audience into truth too deep for human consumption. Apart from the grace of God, this powerful wave of truth was overwhelming, but Jesus chose not to interrupt its momentum with endearing human-interest stories and tension-releasing humor. He was seriously intense about proclaiming the Word of God.

In an essay titled, 'A Genius and an Apostle,' Søren Kierkegaard complained that many of the preachers in his day were 'affected.' Their intensity was artificial. 'It is bad enough,' Kierkegaard wrote, 'the way they talk in a sugary voice and roll their R's like foreigners, and wrinkle their brow and use violent gestures and ridiculous poses. *But even more pernicious is that their whole way of thinking is affected.* Preachers have become like foolish parents who have to beg, plead, and promise to get their children to obey them.'[13]

Kierkegaard believed that the power of the Word of God was not enhanced, but obscured, by the eloquence and brilliance of a genius. He maintained a qualitative difference between a genius and an apostle. A genius is respected for his or her brilliance, the command of intellect, the inventiveness of his mind and quick assimilation of facts. A genius is an innovator whose abilities are clearly superior to others.' The apostle's value, on the other hand, resides not in his abilities but in the call of God upon his life to proclaim the truth of God. We do not listen to Jesus, Kierkegaard contended, because He is clever or eloquent, but because He is wise—wise with the wisdom of God. We respond to Him because He is the way, the truth, and the life.

---

13 Søren Kierkegaard, *The Present Age and Of the Difference Between A Genius And An Apostle* (New York: Harper & Row, 1962), p. 103.

In the Bread of Life discourse, Jesus felt it was better to turn people off with metaphor and mystery than to lead people on under false pretenses. His radical transformation of felt needs was bound to offend some, even as it was powerful to help others.

Unlike so many today who seem to base their ministry on popularity, Jesus judged effectiveness by faithfulness. He was prepared not only for people to walk away but for people to go deeper. Are we prepared to communicate the gospel as Jesus did? Can we compassionately meet people's needs, declare the gospel without manipulation or compromise, and nurture those who are willing to distinguish between a felt need for positive affirmation and the spiritual need for deliverance? Real evangelism involves discipleship and true confession results in commitment. Richard Lovelace writes:

> We may need to challenge more, and comfort less, in our evangelism and discipleship. We need to make it harder for people to retain assurance of salvation when they move into serious sin... We need to tell some persons who think they have gotten saved to get lost. The Puritans were biblically realistic about this; we have become sloppy and sentimental in promoting assurance under any circumstances.[14]

The meaning and method of Jesus' communication defies any attempt to reduce it to human terms. The description offers no other interpretation than a miracle, in fact a series of *nature* miracles. Jesus feeds the multitude, walks on the sea, and claims to be the bread of life. All three shatter modern notions of what is possible and

---

14   Richard Lovelace, 'Evangelicalism: Recovering a Tradition of Spiritual Depth,' *The Reformed Journal*, September 1990, p. 25.

offend Enlightenment rationality. Skeptical commentators scramble for an explanation. John must mean that Jesus succeeded in challenging everyone to share their food with one another and that there was more than enough bread to go around. They claim that Jesus was walking on the beach and that it only looked like He was walking on the water. And when Jesus said He was bread from heaven, He must have been speaking figuratively. He must mean that His teaching and life example are food for thought.

As we have seen, the Bible uses metaphor, story, narrative, and word to convey its message. Why stop there? What about legend, myth, and fairy tale? If we were to agree with the modern mindset and nature-alone-science, we would be forced to join the ranks of the skeptical crowd listening to Jesus. Then we might conclude that feeding the multitude is a beautiful picture of humanitarianism. Walking on the sea is high drama and eating flesh is only poetic license to make a point. After all is said and done, it really is only a morality play with special props. The moral of the story is that we should care for one another, risk our lives in the adventure of life, and understand that there is more to living than food and drink.

Why do we believe this episode in John's Gospel is true? Why do we believe that Jesus literally and miraculously fed the multitude, that He literally and miraculously walked on the sea, and that He literally and miraculously is the Bread of Life? Unbelief may hide behind the moral of the story, but not for very long. If this story is mainly myth and legend, it is easier to accept great values without it. It is easier to believe that this story about Jesus feeding thousands and claiming to be Bread from Heaven is invented than that it is real history. But then, maybe what we are being asked to believe is not easy. It is *work*, just like

Jesus said it was. 'Do not labor for the food that perishes, but for the food that endures to eternal life, which the Son of Man will give to you... This is the work of God, that you believe in him whom he has sent' (John 6:27, 29).

If the moral of the story rests on myth and legend, the moral itself may be untrue or unreal. There may be no moral behind these allegedly invented stories after all. What if there is no need beyond the hunger in our belly? But does that conclusion ring true with what we know about ourselves?

Why should a biological organism made up largely of water, nitrogen, and carbon want something more? If satisfaction were achieved through food, most Americans would be satisfied, because they have plenty of food. But this hunger for something more is just as real as the hunger for food. Why are we so conscious of a desire which no natural happiness will satisfy? Perhaps, we only imagine this greater need. Maybe we should be more content with the philosophy that says, 'Take life easy; eat, drink and be merry' (Luke 12:19, NIV).

Table grace is *not* as simple as we might have hoped. Consider the table. If anything is known in this equation of table grace it is the table, that piece of furniture with a horizontal surface supported by legs. This solid, sturdy, wooden object affords no mystery. What couldn't be more obvious and straightforward than a table? If anything is as it appears, it is a table, right? Yet scientists tell us differently. What appears solid is literally filled with space; in fact, a table is mainly space. Knock-on-wood density is something of an illusion. The table is made of atoms, each of which has more space than matter. If something as simple as a table can afford so much mystery, how much more does grace afford mystery? If I can believe the scientist, can I trust the Incarnate Son of God?

I will leave it to you to decide whether this hunger for something more is real or not. But as for me, the Bread of Heaven is as real as my daily bread. I agree with Peter: 'Lord, to whom shall we go? You have the words of eternal life, and we have believed, and have come to know, that you are the Holy One of God' (John 6:68-69).

Discussion:

1. How do you see the relationship between physical and spiritual needs?

2. On full stomachs, the people were ready to make Jesus king 'by force.' How did Jesus resist and use the people's expectations to develop His message? How did He move from a physical felt need to the deep-seated spiritual need?

3. Jesus insisted on elaborating powerful metaphors to the breaking point of listener credulity. Are we willing to communicate the gospel of Christ the way Jesus did?

4. Why did the crowd leave? How did Jesus separate admirers from followers?

7

Table Talk

... Jesus entered a village. And a woman named
Martha welcomed him into her house.

Luke 10:38

Opening our homes to Jesus is bound to change our lives
in unexpected ways. If you want Jesus close to you, expect
to be changed in ways that may not immediately impress
you as better. Life may not be as neat and tidy as it once
was. When life is no longer under your control, but under
Jesus' control, expect to feel upset for a while.

As Luke tells us in chapter ten of his Gospel, Martha
was hospitable to Jesus, but she wanted to do things her
way. Her way wasn't necessarily bad; it just didn't work well
with what Jesus had in mind. Like Martha, we tend to treat
Jesus as a guest. We forget that He is the Lord. The key
here is to listen to Jesus. We need to sit down. Be quiet.
And listen to Jesus.

When I was in high school, my parents opened our
home to the Chinese Christian Fellowship, a group of
graduate students at the State University of New York,
from Taiwan, Hong Kong, and China. After a long week
of graduate work, these students liked being together in
a home. Every Friday night we hosted twenty-five to eighty

Chinese students. My parents provided most of the food, and the students led their own program. We had to learn what Asian students liked to eat. At first we made some big mistakes. We started out serving pizza and donuts, two items that Chinese students didn't particularly like back in the 70s (Since then, I have been with many Chinese who love pizza!).

My parents befriended these students and became involved in their lives in ways they never anticipated. Being a graduate student in a foreign land is not easy. Loneliness, financial needs, and academic pressures were common. My parents did a lot of listening and praying. They served as parents-in-residence for quite a few weddings, hosting receptions and helping out in any way they could. Some students were introduced to Christ for the first time in our home. Others followed the Lord Jesus in such exemplary ways that our faith was strengthened.

This hospitality had a profound impact on our family. We re-examined our own faith and commitment. The impact of these brothers and sisters in Christ, who were sincerely seeking God's guidance on major life issues, was significant. My brother met his wife, Sarah, in this fellowship. I spent a year teaching in Taiwan because of an encounter one evening with a visiting speaker, Dr. Paul Han.

I am grateful now that my parents opened our home, but I didn't always feel that way. Some Friday nights I resented the fact that our home was virtually taken over by fifty or more Chinese students. Every room in the house was given over to this hospitality, and I had no place to escape in my own home. I remember coming home from college and acting like Martha of Bethany. One Friday night, I opened my bedroom door and found two graduate students sitting on my bed praying. That was the last straw. No privacy in my very own home. Students praying in *my* bedroom! I was angry at my parents for putting others ahead of *me—their son*. Of course, my slight inconvenience was only for a few hours on Friday night! Looking back, I'm not proud of how I felt or how I expressed myself. I am confessing a sin to you, a sin long forgiven, but that night I was much worse than Martha because I just wanted everyone to leave.

LESSONS ON HOSPITALITY

Jesus' journey to the cross sets the stage for Martha's hospitality and Mary's discipleship. Luke writes, 'When the days drew near for him to be taken up, he set his face to go to Jerusalem' (Luke 9:51). Everything that happened on the way from Galilee to Jerusalem was influenced by Jesus' determination to fulfill the will of the Father. Jesus was fully aware of the suffering that awaited Him in Jerusalem. The route was marked by the cross. Jesus used the circumstances and conversations to teach His disciples about Kingdom-of-God hospitality.

When Jesus and His disciples encountered hostility at a Samaritan village, James and John wanted to call fire down from heaven to destroy the village, but Jesus rebuked them. And when Jesus was approached by potential followers, He laid out the high cost of discipleship. Then Jesus sent out an advance team, seventy-two messengers, to go from village to village announcing the coming Kingdom of God. He sent them out 'like lambs among wolves' (Luke 10:3).

Hospitality was a key factor in these disciples' success. They were on an urgent mission, and they were dependent upon God and the hospitality of strangers to meet their needs. They were to travel light and with a sense of urgency. No backpacks. No long, leisurely, customary greetings along the way. If they were graciously received along the way, they were to receive their host's food and drink with gratitude, and bless the household with a simple message: 'The kingdom of God has come near to you' (Luke 10:9).

On the way, Jesus told the parable of the Good Samaritan (Luke 10:25-37). The parable is of special interest because the disciples were fresh from their experience of either hostility or hospitality as they journeyed through Samaria and Galilee. In some Jewish villages, they had been treated badly. They had been despised like Samaritans. Keep in mind that Jesus defines the neighbor as *anyone* in need, but the surprising twist to this parable is that Jesus chose a Samaritan to illustrate genuine love for a stranger. Those who refused hospitality to the seventy-two disciples were like the Jewish priest and Levite in the parable who ignored the wounded man. In spite of cultural prejudices and excuses, the Samaritan showed compassion for a human being. He disinfected and bandaged the wounds of a total stranger, and put him on his donkey. He took him to an inn that would care for the wounded man and nurse him back to health. The Samaritan covered all the expenses for a neighbor he didn't know. If we were making up this story, we might identify the neighbor-in-need as a Samaritan. Instead, the Samaritan is the one who recognizes the half-dead stranger as a person worthy of compassion and care. The Good Samaritan practiced extreme hospitality.

Luke wants us to take in the big picture. The journey began with Samaritan hostility and Jesus' rebuke against retaliation. This was followed by Jesus' stress on the cost of discipleship: 'No one who puts his hand to the plow and looks back is fit for the kingdom of God' (Luke 9:62). Then, He sent out the disciples two-by-two, like 'lambs among wolves,' on an urgent mission to announce the Kingdom of God. The disciples scattered among the villages, ready for a warm reception but prepared for rejection. The parable of the Good Samaritan caps it all off with a convicting look at what it really means to show mercy.

Luke emphasizes that Jesus is in charge. He is Lord. If it's your testosterone-fueled instinct to call down fire on people who reject you, think again. Listen to Jesus. His pointed rebuke is hard to hear. If you like hype and you're ready to join in on all the excitement of following Jesus, you need to listen to Jesus. Jesus squelches thoughtless enthusiasm: 'Foxes have holes, and birds of the air have nests, but the Son of Man has nowhere to lay his head' (Luke 9:58). If you're a religious tourist on a sightseeing excursion, you had better pay attention to Jesus. His mission trip of salvation and judgment is probably not the adventure you had in mind. If you think neighbor-love is about being nice to nice people, you need to listen to Jesus, because it's all about sacrificial love, my life for yours, the love of the cross. All this is to say, if you think your home is your castle, you're sadly mistaken. When Jesus comes into your life, into your home, things change! You are not your own, you were bought with a price—the price of the cross. All this sets the scene for dinner at Martha's.

TENSION AT THE TABLE

Martha and Mary are better known in the Gospel of John than they are in the Gospel of Luke (John 11:1-44; 12:2). From John we learn that their home is in Bethany, two miles from Jerusalem, and that they and their brother Lazarus were close friends of Jesus. We might be surprised that this little incident made its way into the Gospel of Luke, if it were not for the fact that Luke draws our attention to the role of women as disciples of the Lord. He was also concerned to highlight the practical and relational dynamic of following Jesus. This episode offers a snapshot of the kind of discipleship Jesus commends and approves. An artist might be inclined to paint this picture: Mary is sitting at the feet of Jesus, together with the men, listening to Jesus. She is 'one of the guys.' In the foreground, and out of the circle, stands Martha, with one hand on her hip and another pointing at Mary. Her face looks agitated, scowling. She's provoked.

This story is not about the relative merits of Martha and Mary's personality types. Nor is it about the tension between the contemplative life and the active life. If you are looking for an excuse to get off the church board or quit nursery duty, find another text—if you can. The real question is this: *is the work that we want to do for Jesus the work that Jesus wants?* The tension is between our agenda and His.

We have in mind how things should be done, and when we see somebody doing them differently, we are prone to be judgmental and critical. Martha was well-intentioned and working hard to please Jesus, but her effort got in the way of her faithfulness to Jesus. Martha had more to learn about Jesus than she thought she did. What she didn't know about her special guest was far more than what she knew. When it comes to Jesus, that's true for most of us.

When we treat Jesus like a special guest instead of the Lord, *we* determine how best to honor Jesus. We show hospitality, or whatever else we seek to do for Jesus, according to our likes and dislikes, our cultural background and traditions. Instead of listening to Jesus, we do our own thing. These practices may meet a need in our lives for purpose and significance, but that does not change the fact that these religious habits and customs are prescribed by our culture and tradition, not by Jesus.

People wonderfully saved by the grace of Christ are swept up into religious practices that rob them of the joy of following the Lord Jesus. Their understanding of righteousness is skewed, and their life goals have more to do with their own personal agendas than with a passion for Christ. When years of religion and church attendance don't add up to deeper dependence on God, ethical maturity, and authentic spirituality, it is time for us to re-examine our understanding of Jesus' expectations.

Martha's effort to please Jesus prevented her from listening to Jesus. That's a problem. Unwittingly, she threw off Jesus' easy yoke and burdened herself with the heavy yoke of her own expectations and obligations. Martha did it to herself, just as we do it to ourselves. We bring our own agenda to our Christian service, yet we expect Jesus to be pleased. The tell-tale sign of the Martha syndrome in others is when we have to keep reminding ourselves that they mean well. It is a difficult disorder to diagnose in ourselves. Yet the long-term effect of religious busy-work is serious. For such a little text, the implications of this episode are huge for the church. A church of Martha-types passionately serving Jesus in their own way on their own terms ruins the testimony of the work of Jesus. Doing for others what you would like others to do for you may not be the best policy, especially when it comes to serving Jesus.

One humorous incident comes to mind. Years ago, Virginia and I were living in Toronto. I was teaching full time in a seminary, and I had recently begun serving as a teaching pastor in a small urban church. We had put in a long work week, the kids were fussy, and both of us had colds. It was Friday night, in mid-January, and we were booked to go out for dinner with an older couple in the church. We thought about canceling, but we were concerned that postponing the date might lead to hard feelings.

The plan was for them to come by and pick us up. At 6 p.m. sharp, the doorbell rang, and I went to the door. I answered the door and turned to get our coats, when suddenly there was a crowd of church people at the front door, shouting, 'Surprise!' The door was flung open and in walked more than seventy-five people. Picture it. Most of the church cramming into our very small home with their coats and boots, loaded down with food and folding chairs. They carried in a large chocolate layer cake with '*Welcome To Our Church*' scripted in white frosting, bottles of Coke and bags of chips. They brought the church coffee-maker and tableware. Dear old grandmothers who had braved the winter weather to come out sat on church folding chairs lined up in rows in the living room while little kids ran up and down the stairs. Every conceivable space in our matchbox house was occupied by people ready to party. Virginia and I rushed around trying to help the 'hostesses' get the food on and find the utensils they needed. With a pounding headache, I went upstairs to find some aspirin in the bathroom cabinet, only to find two teenagers sitting on metal chairs in the bathtub eating chocolate cake. It really was an unbelievable evening. The endearing part is that everyone meant well.

That night we had a house full of Marthas who were eager to please and one exhausted pastor. I realize that in telling you this story, you may be thinking that I was a tad ungrateful for my congregation's surprise party. Maybe I should ask my Toronto friends for forgiveness for even sharing this story. They may be feeling the way Martha felt when Jesus challenged her service.

No matter how well-intentioned our service may be, if we are following our own agenda instead of the Master's mission, Jesus is not impressed. In Luke's account, body language tells an interesting story. Martha was on her feet scurrying around, busy with meal preparation, attending to the 'needs' of Jesus and his Entourage. Meanwhile, Mary was sitting at the feet of Jesus, listening to what He had to say. The issue is not *doing* versus *being*, but of *being in the doing*. We ought to keep in mind the line from Jesus' earlier message, when He said, 'This is the work of God, that you believe in him whom he has sent' (John 6:29).

Martha was not impressed with Mary, nor with Jesus, for that matter. Instead of coming to Jesus to learn, she came to Jesus to complain: 'Lord, do you not care that my sister has left me to serve alone? Tell her then to help me.' (Luke 10:40). This is a response worthy of attention, because it goes to the heart of much of the complaining that goes on in the church. In so many words, pastors and church workers complain this way all the time. Missionaries say this kind of thing without any qualms. Under the pretense of asking the Lord of the harvest to send out workers into His harvest fields, pastors and missionaries complain like Martha. Maybe we should go ahead and make Martha's complaint the theme verse for a missions conference or the key verse for the church nominating committee, because it is often the underlying theme: 'Lord, don't you care that I'm all alone, doing the work?'

Embedded in Martha's 'table talk' were four faulty perspectives: (1) She accused Jesus of not caring. (2) She judged Mary for abandoning her to work alone. (3) She presumed to know what was the real work. (4) She ordered Jesus to do what she wanted.

Martha was all worked up, and she was ready to explode. In her own way, she was ready for Jesus to call down fire (Luke 9:54). Her feelings poured out: resentment, abandonment, obsession, and pride. Martha felt she had every right to feel unappreciated and overwhelmed; her cause and her complaint were justified. Martha's premise was simple: she is doing the real work, Mary is shirking her duties, and Jesus needs to back her up. Martha is dedicated to serving Jesus in her own way, and she can't imagine any other way to fulfill the mission.

Why listen to Jesus if you have all the answers? This is a danger, especially for Christians who feel they have heard everything there is to hear about Jesus. They think they know everything about following Jesus, but sadly their Jesus is not the Jesus of the Bible, but a stick-figure Jesus, a cultural icon. We presume to know what Jesus stands for and what Jesus wants, but we have stopped listening to Him.

If Martha had her way, she would have turned Mary into another Martha. This is the sad dynamic that is played out when Martha pastors and the Martha parents and the Martha workers bully and manipulate people into becoming like themselves. The Marys of the world are an endangered species. We can be thankful that Jesus doesn't allow us to control others the way we might like to.

Martha had four faulty perspectives; Jesus responded with four constructive perspectives:

1. Jesus comforted her, calling her by name, 'Martha, dear Martha.' Jesus was neither indifferent to nor dismissive of her, nor was He provoked and curt. He began by reassuring her that He cared deeply for her.

2. Jesus confronted the problem. He identified the tension. The problem was not between Him and Martha, nor was it between Mary and Martha. The cause of the anxiety was within Martha. 'You are anxious and troubled about many things...' Worry fueled

Martha's efforts, and her anxiety was produced by the many things she worried about.

3. Jesus corrected Martha's perspective by comparing her preoccupation with many things with a focus on the one thing. Subtraction was key. 'Martha, Martha, ...but few things are needed—or indeed only one.' Martha had her agenda, but it was not the Lord's agenda for her. She was worried about many things, but she lacked the one thing necessary. Instead of seeking first God's kingdom and His righteousness, she was worrying about a long list of self-induced necessities (Matt. 6:25-34). Jesus sought to replace her many distractions with a single focus. Worship has the power to drive out worry. 'One thing have I asked of the LORD, that will I seek after: that I may dwell in the house of the LORD all the days of my life, to gaze upon the beauty of the LORD and to inquire in his temple' (Ps. 27:4).

4. Jesus commended Mary for choosing what is better. He was not reticent about comparing Martha's way with Mary's way and saying that Mary had chosen the better way. As much as we might chafe at the thought, Jesus uses the people around us to show us what is better. Our pride rebels. We want to be told that our way is as good as or better than our sister's way. It is interesting to note that whereas Martha wanted Jesus to order Mary to work ('Tell her to help me!'), Jesus does not order Martha to choose the one thing. He protects Mary's choice ('Mary has chosen the good portion, which will not be taken away from her'), but He does not dictate Martha's choice. She will have to make that

decision. Jesus wants Martha to respect Mary for the better choice.

Luke wants us to take careful note. Mary has a choice in this matter, and Jesus commends her choice. By choosing to sit with the men and listen to Jesus, she is crossing a cultural boundary. There are plenty of women and men today who struggle with women like Mary. They don't know what to do with women like Mary who sit at the feet of Jesus, who study theology and prepare for a teaching ministry. They react to Mary the way Martha did. They think a woman's place is in the kitchen. Jesus affirmed Mary's choice as a woman to take a seat at the table with the men and learn her theology from the Master. Mary is the ideal picture of hospitality because she attends to the guest and, in so doing, recognizes Jesus as her Lord.

Martha illustrates what we often do to the Christian faith when we subject Jesus to our religious expectations and personal preferences. Well-intentioned but misguided religion imposes on Christianity an agenda that is not of the Lord. But Mary let nothing interfere with her relationship with the Lord. She transcended cultural pressures, gender roles and family concerns to serve the Lord and listen to Jesus.

A Testimony Without Words

One final observation: Mary never said a word. When Martha spoke, Mary kept silent. She let her actions speak for themselves. She did not defend herself. Mary never stopped listening to Jesus.

On Monday morning following a full Sunday, I was working in my study at church, preparing a sermon on this text in Luke when Ernie, one of our church elders, dropped by to see me. A few short weeks ago, Ernie's wife died suddenly and unexpectedly from a viral bacterial infection.

Gracie was deeply loved by our household of faith, and her memorial service was very moving.

I was struck by Ernie's appearance. His eyes were clear. His face was relaxed and expressive with a faint smile. His deep voice was sure, his posture erect. I told him that he hadn't missed a beat. Even though he had lost his wife, on Sunday morning he was there in his usual place, worshiping without distraction. You could sense his focus and almost an insistence on worship. There was an authenticity about his whole demeanor, a holistic holiness that permeated his entire being. One only needed to look at Ernie to hear the Word of God preached without words.

When I began to share with Ernie how much his testimony meant to me, he responded in his resonating voice, 'My children see this, too, you know.' I thought to myself, 'Right, who couldn't see it?' The frequency of Ernie's faithfulness was pitched so high that it was silent to our ears, but so pure it penetrated our hearts. Ernie didn't need words. Everyone knew that Ernie had chosen the one thing and that it would never be taken away from him. We know this because Jesus said so.

DISCUSSION:

1. Hosting a meal for a person you highly respect and want to please greatly can produce pressure. How did Martha's respect for Jesus get in the way of her faithfulness to Jesus?

2. What can those of us who are busy with church work learn from Martha? Are your expectations of what you want to do for Jesus tested by what Jesus wants?

3. What would have happened to Mary if Martha had had her way?

4. How did Jesus answer Martha? If Jesus said this to you, how would you have responded?

8

The Guest

Zaccheus, hurry and come down, for I must stay at
your house today.

Luke 19:5

Jesus was always taking the initiative to relate to people
whom everybody expected him to ignore, and along the
way He made some unexpected house calls. He sat at some
pretty unlikely tables and had meals with people judged
corrupt and sinful, but He always did so on His own terms
and for His own purposes. He defied the conventions of
the world, but remained true to His own convictions. One
critic calls Jesus 'the consummate party animal,' but that la-
bel fails to describe the impact of Jesus' table fellowship on
others.[1] He never condoned their sinful lifestyles, nor did
He ever cease calling for repentance, transformation, and
discipleship. But Jesus invariably met people on *their* home
turf. To switch metaphors, He gladly gave away 'home
court advantage' because He was always true to the gospel wherever He was. Jesus' strategy of evangelism was no
more complicated than the description in Revelation 3:20:

---

1   Craig L. Blomberg, *Contagious Holiness*, p. 102.

'Behold, I stand at the door and knock.

If anyone hears my voice and opens the door,

I will come in to him and eat with him, and he with me.'

When it comes to sharing the gospel of Christ, we have plenty to learn. Jesus' *accessibility to others* and His *accountability to the truth* is the model we want to follow.

STAY IN THE STORY

The story about Zacchaeus is a part of the much larger story of salvation history. This is true of all of our stories as well. Everyone has a story, but only one story redeems our story. It is this greater story that gives depth and meaning to Jesus' mealtime fellowship with Zacchaeus. The Sunday School flannel-graph lesson may be how we remember the story of Zacchaeus, but Luke gives us a new perspective with a wider angle. The Zacchaeus story is a conversion story that may be best told in reverse, working back from Palm Sunday. In the Gospel of Luke, the story of Zacchaeus is the last episode before Jesus' royal entrance into Jerusalem, followed by the parable of the ten minas. This parable is about ten servants who each receive an equal sum of money from their royal master. The first servant returns tenfold the investment. A second servant returns a profit fivefold, but a third servant shows no profit because he hid the money. Needless to say, the master is upset with the unprofitable servant. Jesus told this story to illustrate the foolishness of those who reject the good news of the gospel. The parable looks back to the Zacchaeus story in order to explain Jesus' kingdom investment strategy, and then looks forward to Jesus' rejection at the hands of those who will not allow Him to be king. As Jesus headed for Jerusalem His coming sacrificial death was always on His mind.

If we look at Jesus' encounter with Zacchaeus as an isolated incident, we may miss its true importance. How is it that Zacchaeus, this small-in-stature, big-time crook, climaxes Jesus' journey to Jerusalem? We might even question why Jesus had the time and energy to focus on such an unlikely candidate for conversion. The fact that He did so with such 'hold-everything' deliberation is an indication that Zacchaeus was just the kind of person He intended to invest in for the sake of His kingdom. A person following any other agenda would not have given Zacchaeus the time of day, but Jesus was on a mission, heading to His death, and Zacchaeus was just the kind of person He would give His life for. 'For the Son of Man came to seek and to save the lost' (Luke 19:10).

On His journey to Jerusalem, Jesus told a series of stories that anticipated his encounter with Zacchaeus. This Jewish tax-collector and Roman collaborator is much like the quintessential 'outsider' in the parable of the great banquet. He is the kind of needy person Jesus had in mind when He described the recipients of the master's last-minute invitation to the banquet. Chief tax collectors, who were wealthy and corrupt like Zacchaeus, were not on anyone's kingdom list, but they were on Jesus' (Luke 14:1-24).

In the parable of the lost sheep (Luke 15:3-7), the shepherd leaves the ninety-nine to search for a single lost sheep. Zacchaeus is like that one-in-a-hundred lost sheep. In the parable of the lost coin (Luke 15:8-10), the woman lights a lamp and searches everywhere until she finds her lost coin. Zacchaeus is like that lost coin, and he is like the prodigal son, for whom the father waits in loving expectation for his return (Luke 15:1-32). He can also be compared to the persistent widow who refuses to give up on life until she finds satisfaction (Luke 18:1-8).

The Bible describes Zacchaeus as running ahead and climbing up a sycamore-fig tree to see Jesus as He passes by. Imagine Bill Gates or U2's Bono or Oprah forgetting all about image and being willing to do an otherwise ridiculous thing to catch a glimpse of Jesus. Zacchaeus was not only short but, given his eagerness to see Jesus, he may have also been humble. He is like the taxman in Jesus' parable, seeking mercy, and not like the nose-in-the-air Pharisee (Luke 18:9-14). Zacchaeus is willing to humble himself and become like a child to enter the kingdom of God. Even though he has wealth and power, Zacchaeus acts more like the blind beggar than the rich, young ruler. We picture the rich, young ruler approaching Jesus with an air of confidence, but Zacchaeus is hidden in the leafy, sprawling branches of a fig tree. He is hidden, not because he is ashamed of seeking Jesus, but because he may feel insecure and out of place. He may think that he doesn't belong in the company of Jesus. Although he is a corrupt power-broker, he is honest enough to know that he is hungry for something that neither wealth nor power can satisfy. When he stands up and pledges half of his goods to the poor and promises to return four times the damages to anyone he has defrauded, we are witnessing a conversion. The gospel has begun to transform Zacchaeus' life. Jesus said to him, 'Today salvation has come to this house...' (Luke 19:9).

A JERICHO STORY

This Jericho conversion story reminds us of another Jericho conversion story that took place about a thousand years earlier. And if we allow the apostle Peter to put time in perspective, we may embrace the connection. 'But do not overlook this one fact, beloved, that with the Lord one day is as a thousand years, and a thousand years as one day. The Lord is not slow to fulfill his promise as some count slowness, but is patient toward you, not wishing that any should perish, but that all should reach repentance' (2 Pet. 3:8-9).

Salvation history unites these two conversion stories. The story of Zacchaeus and of Rahab is the story of two people on the outside, people who never expected to be included in the kingdom of God. Rahab was the Jericho prostitute who offered hospitality to the two spies sent by Joshua (Josh. 2:1-24). When the king of Jericho sought to capture the spies, Rahab risked her own life to conceal them. Rahab was willing to risk everything she had for a new way of life that she could hardly have imagined, because she believed that what she had wouldn't last. In this way, she is remarkably like Zacchaeus.

Rahab was ignorant of the Law of God and had been raised in a culture immersed in idolatry and immorality. Her name meant 'arrogance.' For the Israelites, the term 'Rahab' was odious. It was synonymous with demonic power and was the symbolic name for Egypt (see Ps. 89:10; 87:4; Isa. 30:7). But by the mercy of God, Rahab became a believer and one of God's own people. God's grace was extended to this Canaanite prostitute. Rahab faced her fears and trusted in the God of Israel, 'for the LORD your God, he is God in the heavens above and on the earth beneath' (Josh. 2:11). It is significant to note that Rahab's name is recorded in the genealogy of Jesus (Matt. 1:5). She was King David's great-great-grandmother. Rahab gave birth to Boaz, who married Ruth, who gave birth to Obed, David's grandfather. She is the outsider who became an insider because of the mercy of God, just like Zacchaeus. Now, a thousand years later in salvation history, a person equally despised by the people, like Rahab in her day, looks down from his perch in the sycamore-fig tree, hoping to see Jesus.

A Gospel Story

The meeting between Jesus and Zacchaeus was by no means random. Zacchaeus may have thought it was a chance encounter, but Jesus saw it all as God's plan. Divine necessity dictated this dinner as surely as when Abraham entertained three strangers near the great trees of Mamre. Everyone looked down on Zacchaeus, but when Jesus reached the spot, He looked up at him. This may only be an incidental reference, but the image of Zacchaeus looking down and Jesus looking up underscores the humility of the One who made Himself nothing, by taking on the very nature of a servant (Phil. 2:6-11). People despised Zacchaeus, the crooked, little taxman, but Jesus sought him out. They looked down on him, but Jesus looked up to him, not because Zacchaeus was a good man in spite of his greed and corruption, but because Zacchaeus was lost and in need of salvation. Zacchaeus was too short to see above the crowd, and Jesus was too perceptive to lose Zacchaeus in the crowd. In a week, Jesus will be hung on a tree—nailed to a wooden cross for the likes of Zacchaeus and of all sinners.

Zacchaeus was eager to see Jesus, but Jesus matched and exceeded Zacchaeus' eagerness. We don't find the attitude in the Gospels that says, 'If only God wanted to communicate to me half as much as I wanted to hear from him.' Instead, we find God taking the initiative. Jesus related personally to this *persona non grata* taxman. Jesus stopped, looked up, and said, 'Zacchaeus, hurry and come down, for I must stay at your house today.' First he called him by name, just as He had done with His original disciples. This must have surprised Zacchaeus, who undoubtedly thought that Jesus didn't even know he existed. Then, Jesus related to Zacchaeus decisively. 'Hurry and come down' is not the kind of thing you say to someone you are reluctant to meet. Howard Marshall notes that 'Behind Jesus' summons lies a necessity imposed on him by God; the implication is that a divine plan is being worked out.'[2] Under divine necessity Jesus invites Himself to be a guest in Zacchaeus' home.

For his part, Zacchaeus did exactly as he was told. He came down the tree and welcomed Jesus gladly. Without stanzas of 'Just as I am' sung in the background or any special effects or clever incentives, Zacchaeus was ready, even eager, to respond. The crowd put its spin on this unexpected turn of events. They muttered, 'He has gone in to be the guest of a man who is a sinner' (Luke 19:7).

Hobnobbing with a greedy little power-broker like Zacchaeus would have only confirmed the judgment of cynical skeptics who condemned Jesus for being 'a glutton and a drunkard, a friend of tax collectors and sinners' (Matt. 11:19). The crowd was hostile to the hospitality of Jesus. But Zacchaeus 'welcomes Jesus into his home and he does so with joy, since the coming of Jesus to share his home is a sign of fellowship and ultimately of forgiveness.'[3] The crowd, on the other hand, concludes that for Jesus 'to stay in such a person's home was tantamount to sharing in his sin.'[4] These two perspectives are diametrically opposed. Is Jesus legitimizing Zacchaeus' lifestyle by desiring his hospitality and table fellowship? Or is Jesus showing compassion not only for the down and out, but for the up and out, as well? What follows is very important for resolving the conflict of these two perspectives.

---

2   I. Howard Marshall, *The Gospel of Luke*, p. 697.

3   Ibid.

4   Ibid.

A Conversion Story

There is much that goes unsaid in this encounter. Commentators debate whether there was any table fellowship at all. However, from the time Jesus entered Zacchaeus' house as 'the guest of a sinner', to the time Zacchaeus 'stood up', we assume that the two men shared a meal together. It is also safe to assume that Jesus' work and words shape Zacchaeus' response. From all that Jesus has said about poor widows, self-righteous Pharisees, rich, young rulers, Good Samaritans and repentant tax collectors, we are not surprised that Jesus reached out to Zacchaeus. Nor are we surprised by Zacchaeus' testimony. Craig Blomberg observes,

> Jesus so cares for those rightly or wrongly stigmatized by society that he ignores the conventional restrictions on intimately associating with them. He is willing to go to their homes. Indeed, here he insists on it. He shares their food and lodging, but he never does so simply for inclusiveness' sake. A call to repentance is always implicit unless, as here, the individual in question takes the initiative to declare his change of heart and behavior.[5]

The good news is not inclusiveness for inclusiveness' sake, nor is it tolerance for tolerance's sake. There is an 'in the world, but not of the world' tension in this situation. For Zacchaeus to have truly received Jesus and remained unchanged would have been impossible. No one can come to Jesus and remain the same. We come as we are, but we will never remain as we were. The earnest, rich, young ruler tried coming to Jesus, but ended up leaving because he couldn't part with his wealth. When Jesus said, 'How

---

5   Craig L. Blomberg, *Contagious Holiness*, p. 156.

difficult it is for those who have wealth to enter the kingdom of God! For it is easier for a camel to go through the eye of a needle than for a rich person to enter the kingdom of God,' the disciples reacted. Bewildered, they asked, 'Then who can be saved?' Jesus replied, 'What is impossible with men is possible with God' (Luke 18:24-27). In the Bread of Life discourse, Jesus made a similar point, 'No one can come to me unless the Father who sent me draws him...' (John 6:44).

The disciples commented on one type of impossibility, namely, a wealthy person acknowledging his real need for God and then willingly giving up his wealth and following Jesus. The crowd picks up on this same impossibility, but from another angle. They can't imagine Zacchaeus changing because of Jesus; they can only imagine Jesus changing because of Zacchaeus. They imagine the power to corrupt to be greater than the power to transform. They thought it was impossible to associate with someone like Zacchaeus without becoming like him. They jumped to the conclusion that Jesus was showing His true colors.

In many Christian circles today, people like Zacchaeus are a target, not because they are lost, but because they are rich. People in the 'Jesus Business' search out religious consumers and try to sell them a product. In this kind of transaction, radical transformation is on no one's agenda. Leaders in the 'Jesus Business' pride themselves on being able to 'handle' people like Zacchaeus. They provide religious services that build self-esteem, positive spirituality, and personal reassurance, and in return, these consumers write a substantial check. The wealthy are made to feel important because they are large contributors. However, coming to Jesus is different to participating in the 'Jesus Business'. We cannot come to Jesus and remain as we are. *Non-conversion* is impossible. The difference between a dejected, rich, young ruler and a radically converted Zacchaeus is huge.

Zacchaeus' testimony evidenced a complete transformation. Instead of Jesus becoming defiled by eating with Zacchaeus, Zacchaeus became redeemed by eating with Jesus. Contagious holiness overwhelmed infectious impurity. When Zacchaeus stood up from the table, he spoke from the bottom of his heart. 'Look, Lord! Here and now I give half of my possessions to the poor, and if I have cheated anybody out of anything, I will pay back four times the amount.'(Luke 19:8 NIV) Implicit in Zacchaeus' act of restitution were the attributes of true conversion, humility, repentance, sorrow, and sacrifice. Zacchaeus was not trying to earn his salvation, or buy his way into the kingdom, but he was responding to the salvation received in Jesus. Filled with a powerful sense of God's mercy and forgiveness, he was putting his money where his heart was. The meaning of conversion is eloquently expressed by the apostle Paul, who says,

> For by grace you have been saved through faith. And this is not your own doing; it is the gift of God, not a result of works, so that no one may boast. For we are his workmanship, created in Christ Jesus for good works, which God prepared beforehand, that we should walk in them. (Eph. 2:8-10)

Zacchaeus embodied the real-world consequences of saving faith. Many Christians cling to a very limited understanding of evangelism. They stress the simple gospel message and little else: Jesus died for our sins, and whoever accepts Him as their personal Savior will have everlasting life. Unfortunately, this narrow understanding of evangelism tends to produce an emotional conversion that leaves much of the old nature intact. Evangelism is reduced to inviting people to church for a brief presentation of the gospel followed by an emotional appeal to make a decision. What is sadly neglected in this presentation of the gospel is Jesus' understanding of the Kingdom of God. We have in Zacchaeus an example of a person who is working out the meaning of saving faith.

Faith in Christ is demonstrated through the works of faith. We are saved by faith alone, but saving faith is never alone. In the words of the Reformers, 'Faith alone justifies, but not the faith that is alone.' Luther said it well: 'True faith will no more fail to produce good works than the sun can cease to give light.' Faith without works is cheap grace. It is useless, dead faith. Those who live by it are trusting in a religious illusion, a grace they bestow on themselves. True faith overcomes the inertia of indifference, the rationalizations, the unending calculations and the safe retreat into our own cocoon. Rhetoric without costly service undermines the faith as quickly as any heretical idea ever could.

Unlike the rich, young ruler, Zacchaeus stepped up to the challenge of following Jesus, and Jesus commended him for his faith. In an authoritative pronouncement that matched and exceeded Zacchaeus' announcement, Jesus proclaimed, 'Today salvation has come to this house, since he also is a son of Abraham. For the Son of Man came to seek and to save the lost' (Luke 19:9-10). These two sentences are filled with significance for those familiar with salvation history. They recall the day the prophets foretold when people would turn to God from their wicked ways. They recall the covenant that God made with Abraham over their working lunch. They recall the Lord's promise to be the good shepherd who comes to search for and save the lost sheep of Israel. If anyone capitalized on the investment strategy Jesus outlined in the parable of the ten minas, it was Jesus. Zacchaeus was just the kind of person He came to save. He was a person like us, because we 'all have sinned and fall short of the glory of God' (Rom. 3:23).

The church that follows the Lord Jesus will follow His investment strategy. We are called to extend His invitation to all those, like Zacchaeus, who are in real need of radical conversion. To do so, we need the confidence, courage and humility of Jesus to invite ourselves into people's lives for the sake of the Kingdom and their salvation. We may risk the crowd's disapproval and the appearance of contamination, but the benefit is the contagious holiness of Jesus.

DISCUSSION:

1. There is a difference between religious consumers and true seekers. If Zacchaeus had been a consumer, rather than a seeker, what would he have wanted Jesus to do?

2. The people's comment, 'He has gone to be the guest of a sinner,' was not a simple statement of fact, but an indictment against Jesus. Guilt by association has a long history. Why did Jesus insist on table fellowship despite the people's opinion?

3. Instead of Jesus becoming defiled by eating with Zacchaeus, Zacchaeus became redeemed by eating with Jesus. How did contagious holiness overcome infectious impurity?

4. Jesus' insistence on table fellowship with Zacchaeus was not designed to offend the victims of tax abuse. How does Jesus' final statement (Luke 19:10) clarify His motivation?

9

The Family Meal

For who is greater, one who reclines at table or one
who serves? Is it not the one who reclines at table?
But I am among you as the one who serves.

Luke 22:27

Ever since Abraham served roasted lamb to his three visitors
and Moses presided over the Passover meal, salvation
history has been moving to this meal above all meals. The
Last Supper is the climax of God's table fellowship and the
divine invitation to hospitality. At the Last Supper Jesus is
host to three meals in one. First, the meaning of this meal
is rooted in the Passover, which has a long history of being
the ultimate family meal. '...Every man shall take a lamb
according to their fathers' houses, a lamb for a household.
And if the household is too small for a lamb, then he and
his nearest neighbor shall take according to the number
of persons; according to what each can eat you shall make
your count for the lamb' (Exod. 12:3-4). Second, the Last
Supper, the meal that Jesus had with His disciples on the
night that He was betrayed, is the ultimate sacrificial meal.
'For as often as you eat this bread and drink the cup, you
proclaim the Lord's death until he comes' (1 Cor. 11:26).
Finally, the Last Supper is a farewell meal. 'I have earnestly
desired to eat this Passover with you before I suffer. For

I tell you I will not eat it until it is fulfilled in the kingdom of God' (Luke 22:15-16). This ultimate sacrificial family meal is eaten in anticipation of the glorious reunion at the marriage supper of the Lamb. 'Blessed are those who are invited to the marriage supper of the Lamb!' (Rev. 19:9). This eucharistic family meal has a past, present and future in salvation history. As far as the followers of Christ are concerned, this is the meal that is absolutely essential for table grace.

CHRIST'S FAMILY MEAL

When we consider the Last Supper in its context, it looks and feels a whole lot more like an honest-to-goodness family meal than a boring religious ritual that prolongs a church service. Family meals are always intentional. Someone goes to a lot of work to put on a meal. Somebody has to plan the menu, purchase the food, prepare the meal, set the table, and insist on attendance. Someone has to set the tone, establish order, and encourage dialogue. Around the family table we are equal. We may not be equally mature or equally gifted or even equally accountable for the well-being of the family, but we are all equal members of the family. No one has more of a right to sit at the table than another.

We not only bring an appetite to supper, we bring an attitude. We are hungry for more than food. I like to think of our kitchen table as the table of the Lord. This is where we meet for most of our discussion, debate, humor, prayer, and sharing of God's Word. This is where a hunger and thirst for righteousness is felt and prayed over. We probably do more arguing and more affirming around the kitchen table than we do anywhere else. Dining well is a family tradition that takes skill. It involves preparation and planning, scheduling and prioritizing.

We go to a lot of work to put on a good meal. But the preparation that has gone into Christ's family meal is almost unfathomable. Nothing less than the grand sweep of salvation history stands behind this meal. At the Last Supper Jesus looks after everything. He gives directions to Peter and John to prepare for the Passover in a large room that He has arranged to be used. He washes the disciples' feet, serves the meal, sets the tone, carries the conversation and concludes the meal with a blessing. Jesus is still doing what only He can do—'You prepare a table before me in the presence of my enemies' (Ps. 23:5). What the psalmist imagined figuratively, Jesus performed literally. Jesus gives us His body and blood. From start to finish, Jesus looks after the meal. The setting, the preparations and the conversation are all under His supervision. He is the host who arranges everything. He is the servant who washes the disciples' feet. He is both High Priest and Passover Lamb. He is the bread and the cup. The Last Supper is the family meal of all family meals. Yet, as Eugene Peterson has noted, 'Given the prominence of the Supper in our worshiping lives, the prominence of meals in the Jesus work of salvation, it is surprising how little notice is given among us to the relationship between the Meal and our meals.'[1]

TENSION-FILLED FAMILY MEAL

The seventh meal in the Gospel of Luke is the Last Supper. Table grace has been building to this point. The first meal is described as a great banquet hosted by Levi, the tax collector (Luke 5:29-32). The Pharisees complained to the disciples, 'Why do you eat and drink with tax collectors and sinners?' Jesus answered them, 'Those who are well have no need of a physician, but those who are sick. I have

---

1   Eugene H. Peterson, *Christ Plays in Ten Thousand Places*, p. 215.

not come to call the righteous but sinners to repentance.' The second meal was hosted by a Pharisee who became offended when Jesus did not reject, but encouraged, the affection and reverence of a woman with a sinful reputation (Luke 7:36-50). Jesus challenged Simon the Pharisee and extended forgiveness to the woman. The third meal was the miracle of feeding the multitude (Luke 9:12-17), which was followed by the crowd's rejection of Jesus' hospitality because they couldn't stomach His message: 'Unless you eat the flesh of the Son of Man and drink his blood, you have no life in you' (John 6:53). The fourth meal was the meal hosted by Martha (Luke 10:38-42). The fifth meal was hosted by a Pharisee who was offended that Jesus did not wash before the meal, prompting Jesus to come down hard on all the Pharisees for their hypocrisy (Luke 11:37-54). The sixth meal was hosted by a Pharisee who was offended that Jesus healed on the Sabbath (Luke 14:1-24). Tension appears to be a major factor in every meal described in Luke's Gospel. The seventh meal was the Last Supper, and there was plenty of tension around this table as well.

If there ever was a meal situated in the presence of enemies, it was this one. Luke makes sure we feel the strain and suspense that existed outside and inside the upper room. This was a family meal that was characterized by anxiety and fear. The religious leaders were looking 'for some way to get rid of Jesus' (NIV), which they could have done easily if it had not been for the people's respect for Jesus. Judas Iscariot, the ultimate insider, provided the break the religious leaders were looking for. 'Then Satan entered into Judas called Iscariot... He went away and conferred with the chief priests and officers how he might betray him to them' (Luke 22:3-4).

Luke alone of the Gospel writers attributed Satanic influence to Judas (Luke 22:3). Matthew quoted Jesus' pointed remark, 'Truly, I say to you, one of you will betray me,' which disturbed and grieved the disciples (Matt. 26:21). And who could blame them? Jesus' allegation put everyone on notice. His reference to *one of you* required self-examination for everyone.

Matthew made it clear that Jesus loved Judas to the end. Jesus' confrontation with Judas showed great care and timing. First, He removed the veil of secrecy without exposing Judas to the other disciples. He protected Judas' privacy, yet at the same time uncovered his anonymity.[2] Jesus confronted Judas indirectly, letting Judas know that He knew what he was conspiring to do. But He did this without explicitly outing Judas. This prevented the other disciples from ganging up on him. What Jesus did for Judas in conversation, the Holy Spirit does for us in our conscience. Judas was made aware of his sinful intentions (John 16:8). He was carefully exposed.

Secondly, Jesus mercifully warned him: 'This cup that is poured out for you is the new covenant in my blood. But behold, the hand of him who betrays me is with me on the table. For the Son of Man goes as it has been determined, but woe to that man by whom he is betrayed!' (Luke 22:20-22). Matthew added, 'It would be better for that man if he had not been born' (Matt. 26:24). As R.T. France observes, 'Since the meal was eaten from a common dish into which all those present would frequently dip their hands, this is no more specific identification than verse 21.'[3] Jesus chose an image that underscored the intimacy of His fellowship with Judas in conjunction with a warning that clarified the true nature of the evil contemplated by Judas. Jesus made sure that there was no way Judas could understand his evil plan to be anything other than the betrayal of the Son of

---

2   Frederick Dale Bruner, *Matthew 13-28: The Churchbook*, p. 612.

3   R. T. France, *Matthew* (Grand Rapids: Eerdmans, 1985), p. 367.

Man. Furthermore, Jesus rested in the full sovereignty of God ('The Son of Man will go just as it is written about him') and declared the full responsibility of His betrayer ('But woe to that man who betrays the Son of Man!'). 'The events must happen *as it is written*; but this does not excuse deliberate betrayal.'[4]

Thirdly, Jesus extended to Judas the freedom to betray Him. After having exposed and warned him, Jesus said to him in effect, 'I know who you are, and I'm not stopping you.' Matthew informs us that Judas feigned ignorance and innocence: 'You don't mean me, do you, Rabbi?' Note that each one of the disciples said, 'Surely not I, Lord?' but Judas addressed Jesus as *Rabbi*. In contrast to the title, 'Lord,' Judas used the title 'Rabbi' to subtly limit his respect for Jesus. Even while pretending to be innocent, Judas revealed his resentment against the stature of Jesus and sent his own indirect message to Jesus. Jesus answered Judas more obliquely than most English versions translate. Jesus in effect said, 'If you say so' or 'Those are your words.' He gave Judas neither a 'yes' nor a 'no,' but answered him in such a way as to challenge his implicit denial and prearranged betrayal.

The dialogue between Jesus and Judas is evidence that Jesus loved Judas in spite of his wickedness. Jesus exposed him carefully, warned him thoughtfully, and gave him the leeway to act according to the evil dictates of his heart. Judas not only had the freedom to betray Jesus, he had the freedom to confess, repent, and turn to Jesus. Jesus gave Judas three chances to change his mind, reverse course, and accept the gospel. John Calvin wrote, 'In the person of Judas the Lord wished His people in all ages to be warned.'[5]

---

4   R. T. France, *Matthew* p. 367.

5   John Calvin, *A Harmony of the Gospels: Matthew, Mark, and Luke, 3 vols.* (1555, ed. 1972), quoted in Bruner, *Matthew: The Churchbook*, p. 617.

Luke's Gospel emphasizes that it was not only the re-ligious leaders and Judas who contributed to the tension around the table at the Last Supper; all the disciples played a part. 'A dispute also arose among them, as to which of them was to be regarded the greatest' (Luke 22:24). Of all times for a fight to break out over which of them was the greatest, this had to be the worst—they had just celebrated the meal together!

Everywhere we look in this situation, there was some form of evil to contend with. There was outside opposition from the religious authorities, insider betrayal, negative group dynamics and sinful self-confidence. Jesus even had to call Simon to account, exposing his false bravado and self-deception. No doubt about it, this was a tension-filled family meal. Everyone made this meal difficult except the host.

THE CALMNESS OF JESUS

Jesus fulfilled the psalmist's famous line, 'You prepare a table before me in the presence of my enemies.' At the Last Supper there were enemies without and enemies within. Every kind of evil surrounded this table fellowship: hatred, pride, self-righteousness, deception, betrayal, and denial. Darrell Bock writes:

> Everything about this event reflects the calmness of Jesus and the control of God present in the activity. Jesus directs all the activity, knowing how each detail will fall into place. Though the Passover meal is being celebrated, in another sense the Passover Lamb is preparing to offer himself after this one last meal with his disciples. Nothing catches him by surprise.[6]

6   Darrell L. Bock, *Luke: The NIV Application Commentary* (Grand Rapids: Zondervan, 1996), p. 552.

In the midst of all of the stress, anxiety and confusion, someone remained calm. We are not surprised that it was Jesus. As we read over this passage, our minds and hearts focus on the tension in the text. But note carefully the many ways that the calmness of the Lord is evident. There was never any doubt as to who was in charge. Everything happened in an orderly fashion. The timing, location and preparation for celebrating the Passover meal were under Jesus' control. He saved His anguished thoughts for Gethsemane—for His communion with the Father—but in the upper room with His disciples, He was in control and calm. His leadership prevailed in the midst of the storm.

There was never any doubt as to how He felt. 'I have earnestly desired to eat this Passover with you before I suffer' (Luke 22:15). And even though the disciples caused so much grief around this table with their bickering about who was the greatest, Jesus persisted in loving them, teaching them, building them up and preparing them for what was coming. Jesus began the evening by washing the disciples' feet, a startling example of His love for them (John 13:1-11).

There was never any doubt as to the meaning of the meal. He set forth clearly that this was a sacrificial meal. 'And he took bread, and when he had given thanks, he broke it and gave it to them, saying, "This is my body, which is given for you. Do this in remembrance of me." And likewise the cup after they had eaten, saying, "This cup that is poured out for you is the new covenant in my blood"' (Luke 22:19-20).

There was never any doubt in His mind about who was going to betray Him, yet Jesus was calm about the events that were about to transpire. He went from 'the words of institution' to the words of confrontation. '...The hand of him who betrays me is with me on the table' (Luke 22:21). Jesus was able to talk calmly about Judas.

There was never any doubt in His mind about the human condition. Jesus was not surprised or exasperated by the disciples' argument over who was the greatest. Instead, He turned it into a teaching opportunity.

There was never any doubt in His mind about the future. In spite of the disciples' ineptitude, Jesus took the opportunity to offer His blessing and confirm the Father's will. '...I assign to you, as my Father assigned to me, a kingdom, that you may eat and drink at my table in my kingdom and sit on thrones judging the twelve tribes of Israel' (Luke 22:29-30). Amidst the small-minded preoccupations of the disciples, Jesus focused on the big picture of the future.

There was never any doubt in His mind that Peter would be restored to complete fellowship in spite of his denials. 'Simon, Simon, behold, Satan demanded to have you, that he might sift you like wheat, but I have prayed for you that your faith may not fail' (Luke 22:31-32). Unmoved by Peter's egotistical self-confidence, Jesus was able to talk calmly about Peter's denials.

Jesus embodied in Himself the attitude called for in the first Passover meal. The Israelites were instructed: 'Be fully dressed with your sandals on and your stick in your hand. Eat in a hurry; it's the Passover to GOD' (Exod. 12:11 MSG).

THREE MEALS IN ONE
The Last Supper is a family meal, a sacrificial meal and a farewell meal. All three dimensions are important in this one meal, but it is important to remember that it is only this one meal that the church has to offer. One popular American pastor suggests that an effective church is more like a restaurant than a home:

It is wonderful to have a home-cooked meal—but you would never go to another person's house to eat it unless first invited. Even if you had a good time, you can't forget that you are an outsider—all the family members know one another very well; they have regular places to sit; they have an inside humor you don't always catch; and when the meal is over, they stay and you leave. Everything is on their terms, not yours. A restaurant is different. Restaurants cater to outsiders. They exist for outsiders. Customers get the best tables, set their own schedule, and leave when they choose. Same food, but different stories.[7]

I suppose the church could model itself after the shopping mall food court, but it is a temptation we should avoid. We don't have a menu designed around everyone's tastes. Many people want a spirituality customized according to their likes and dislikes, but that is not what the Lord offers. The Lord's Supper is not immediately accessible, and it is not whatever we want it to be. We have to pay attention to Jesus if we are going to get in on its true meaning. There are strange tensions around the table. The world is invited to this table—'whosoever will may come,'—but everyone who comes must submit to what this table offers. The host is in charge, and it is the meal we need to eat. Jesus offers the bread and the wine, His body and blood, for the eternal nourishment of our everlasting life, and His banner over us is love (Song 2:4). At the beginning and at the end of this meal, Jesus reminded His disciples that His next meal with them would be at the Great Banquet, the Marriage Supper of the Lamb. 'For I tell you I will not eat it until it is fulfilled in the kingdom of God' (Luke 22:16).

---

7   Leith Anderson, *A Church for the 21st Century* (Minneapolis, Minnesota: Bethany House, 1992), p. 116.

DISCUSSION:

1. If there ever was a meal situated 'in the presence of our enemies', it was this one. Identify the difficulties and tensions surrounding this meal. Are you willing to meet Jesus in the midst of your life's tensions?

2. How did Jesus host the Last Supper? How did He lead? What did He teach? If you were seated at that table, how would you have felt?

3. Is there a eucharistic sensibility to your family meal? How can we practice Jesus' spiritual discipline of calmness?

4. Why is it important for table grace to be defined by the Last Supper rather than the shopping mall food court?

10

Breakfast on the Beach

Jesus said 'Come and have breakfast.' Now none of
the disciples dared ask him, 'Who are you?' They
knew it was the Lord. Jesus came and took the bread
and gave it to them, and so with the fish.

John 21:12-13

Nietzsche quipped, 'You will have to look more redeemed if
I am to believe in your redeemer.' But I doubt if the tortured
philosopher of despair was in any way impressed by a life
of quiet faithfulness, deep faith, true worship and real love.
After the resurrection, when life returns to normal, the
apostle John shows us what authentic faith and trust in the
risen Lord looks like. The person who helps us see this most
clearly is Peter. And what we discover is that believers in
the risen Lord Jesus look and act pretty normal. In the eyes
of the world, *and in their own eyes*, Christians are not very
special. In the last chapter of the Gospel of John, we are
given a picture of the new normal. We learn that humility,
genuine dependence on God, and life-risking obedience
are by God's design. We come to understand that 'a saint is
never consciously a saint—a saint is consciously dependent
on God.'[1]

---

1   Oswald Chambers, *My Utmost for His Highest* (New York: Dodd, Mead &
     Company, 1966), reading for November 15, p. 320.

Chapter 20 of John's Gospel makes for a good ending. Everything appears to be wrapped up nicely. We are given a brief but *total* picture of the Easter Story. The tomb is empty, and the risen Lord Jesus appears first to Mary Magdalene and then to the disciples. The risen Lord commissions the disciples and offers them the Holy Spirit. He authorizes them to proclaim the gospel. He confronts Thomas' skepticism, and the doubting disciple is convinced. Thomas exclaims, 'My Lord and my God!' Chapter 20 closes with what sounds like the conclusion to the entire book: 'Now Jesus did many other signs in the presence of the disciples, which are not written in this book; but these are written so that you may believe that Jesus is the Christ, the Son of God, and that by believing you may have life in his name' (John 20:30-31).

Yet the Spirit convinced the apostle John that one more vital perspective was needed. Chapter 21 sets forth what the risen Lord Jesus expects of His disciples—of all of His disciples. What does the follower of Jesus Christ look like? What should the world expect to find in the believing community? John's final chapter provides an accurate picture of the honest believer. He describes the new normal.

THE REPRESENTATIVE DISCIPLE

Some might argue that Peter was a more exciting and inspiring person *before* the cross and the resurrection of Jesus than he was after. From the beginning, he appears to be our representative. The gospel narrative focuses on Peter. He is the disciple we can identify with. Whenever the disciples are listed in the Gospels, his name heads the list. He appears to be the disciples' spokesman, asking the questions and speaking up on their behalf. On occasion, he tried unsuccessfully to take charge of Jesus' public relations by managing the Master's movements and controlling access. Of all the disciples, we see his heart the most. He reminds us of ourselves when he drops to his knees and says, 'Go away from me, Lord; I am a sinful man!' (Luke 5:8, NIV).

Peter was the first to confess Jesus as Lord and the first to pledge his unwavering loyalty to Jesus. In the upper room, when Jesus sought to wash the disciples' feet, it was Peter who made a scene and said, 'You shall never wash my feet' (John 13:8). Peter dramatically vowed that he would die before ever denying Jesus. He boasted, 'Though they all fall away because of you, I will never fall away' (Matt. 26:33). In the Garden of Gethsemane, Peter took matters into his own hands. He defended Jesus by drawing his knife and cutting off the ear of one of the arresting officers.

You could always count on Peter to display two distinctive character qualities: 'devotion to Jesus and resistance to Jesus' role as the one who lays down his life for his disciples.'[2] This pattern was set early on when Peter followed up his bold confession, 'You are the Christ, the Son of the living God,' with his flat-out rebuke, 'Never, Lord!' after Jesus spoke of the cross (Matt. 16:16, 22, NIV). Peter got the confession right, but he had no idea what it meant to be committed to the crucified and risen Lord. He was simultaneously devoted and resistant.

And who can forget that moment in the courtyard outside of the house of the high priest? After Peter uttered his third denial and he heard the rooster crow, Jesus turned and looked straight at him. Peter remembered what Jesus had said, and he went outside and wept bitterly. We take for granted Peter's wounded soul, but this narrative detail is significant. In late antiquity, recording a poor

---

2   Timothy Wiarda, *Interpreting Gospel Narratives: Scenes, People, and Theology* (Nashville, Tennessee: B&H, 2010), p. 21.

man's feelings was rarely done. We have become used to it, 'because we are the heirs of a culture that, in a sense, sprang from Peter's tears.'[3] We take for granted that a human person, even a Galilean peasant, has an intrinsic dignity and eternal value. The bedrock conviction that each and every ordinary human being is of infinite worth was a foreign concept in antiquity and would be in our own day, if it were not for Jesus Christ.

Before the cross and the resurrection, Peter was a man full of action and charisma. Among the disciples, he was first among equals. He projected a strong, confident self-image. By all accounts, he was an inspiring, dynamic character. But he was also a man full of himself. Everyone agrees that the man who showed up on Pentecost to preach the first Easter message was a very different man than the one who repeatedly tried to master the Master. What changed?

A Modest Meal

The Gospel of John ends with breakfast on the beach followed by a conversation (John 21). The disciples left Jerusalem and returned to their homes in Galilee. Seven of them went fishing: Peter, Thomas, Nathanael, James, John, and two unnamed disciples. Everything about the occasion, the place, the work, the people, and the timing was ordinary. In this setting, the disciples are doing exactly what they were doing three years earlier when Jesus first called them to be His disciples. He said to Peter, 'There is nothing to fear. From now on you'll be fishing for men and women' (Luke 5:10, MSG). All seven were radically changed by Jesus, but they didn't look any different. Their personalities were much the same as they had been. But

---

3   David Bentley Hart, *Atheist Delusions: The Christian Revolution and Its Fashionable Enemies* (New Haven: Yale University Press, 2009), p. 167.

think of all that they had been through, all that they had seen and heard and experienced. They were friends. They were fishermen, and they still needed to eat, so they went fishing.

The only one standing on that beach who was special was the risen Lord; everyone else was quite ordinary. Jesus was on the shore, and they were on the water fishing, when He began the conversation. He called out to them, 'Children, do you have any fish?' They answered, 'No.' Fishing all night may have been the disciples' attempt to return to normal. Being together and doing what they knew best how to do was all part of dealing with their grief and confusion. Having worked all night, their empty nets were no doubt sadly symbolic of how they must have felt—empty.

In the morning, they were hungry and tired. Jesus stood on shore, but they didn't recognize Him. In response to Jesus' question, 'Do you have any fish?' one single word summed up life: 'No.' Then Jesus said, 'Cast the net on the right side of the boat, and you will find some.' When they did as He said, 'they were not able to haul it in, because of the quantity of fish.' John immediately knew who was standing on the shore. He said to Peter, 'It is the Lord!' And as we might have expected, Peter jumped into the water. His walking-on-water days were over. He did a 'cannon-ball' and headed for shore. They were about a hundred yards from Jesus (the length of a football field). Peter swam to shore as the six other disciples rowed to shore dragging the net full of fish.

On the beach, Jesus had a charcoal fire going, and he was roasting some fish. The Host had some fresh bread there as well. 'Bring some of the fish that you have just caught,' Jesus said to the seven disciples. In such a natural and ordinary setting it was hard for the disciples to believe that this was really Jesus and that this was actually happening. They wanted to ask, 'Who are you?' but they didn't dare. They knew it was Him, but they could hardly believe it. Jesus was so real, right there in Galilee, eating with them, by the Sea of Tiberias. Once again, the ordinary was juxtaposed with the extraordinary. Jesus was in their world—in their fishing, eating, working, and relating world. If there was to be another appearance by the risen Lord, they did not expect it to be in Galilee. Jerusalem was the heart of the world and the place where the Messiah would be revealed. No wonder they were struggling to come to terms with this experience.[4] Think of it: Jesus around your kitchen table, in the food court at the mall, around the lunch table at work. The risen Lord Jesus encounters us in our everyday world, where we live and work and relate.

Spiritual Supersizing

Traditionally, Christians have resisted the meaning of this down-to-earth breakfast on the beach. For starters, this may be one of the most criticized fishing trips of all time. Some commentators have gone so far as to say that the disciples committed apostasy. Instead of remaining true to their calling, they returned to their old habits and routines. Had they forgotten that Jesus said, 'No one who puts his hand to the plow and looks back is fit for service in the kingdom of God' (Luke 9:62)? Other critics have said that, at the very least, the fishing trip showed the disciples to be aimless and somewhat desperate about what to do next.

What is overlooked in this criticism is that the disciples needed to eat. They still had to provide food for their families and themselves. There was nothing rebellious or

---

4   George R. Beasley-Murray, *John: Word Biblical Commentary*, Vol. 36 (Waco, Texas: Word Books, 1987), p. 399.

unspiritual about their wanting to go fishing. We don't need to make the disciples more spiritual than God intended them to be.

Commentators have felt the need to find some value-added significance in this episode, as if the presence of the risen Lord Jesus was not special enough. According to Augustine, the number seven—the number of disciples present—is an indication of the end of time. The sea is a picture of the world, and the shore of the end of the world. The large haul of fish dragged to shore represents the 'thousands of saints who have shared in the grace of the Spirit.' The definite number of fish is significant as well. It is made up of the number ten, which stands for the Ten Commandments, plus the number seven, which represents the Holy Spirit. The total is seventeen, and when the numbers are added up consecutively from one to seventeen, the total is 153. Thus, the number stands for the fulfillment of the Law through the work of the Holy Spirit.

Augustine wasn't finished uncovering the secret significance of this episode. The roasted fish is the suffering Christ, the bread is the Bread of Life come down from heaven, and the seven disciples are the universal community of believers. Moreover, in the conversation between Jesus and Peter, Augustine tries to explain why Peter loved the Lord more than any of the other disciples and why John was loved by the Lord more than Peter. Augustine's exercise in over-thinking creates an interpretative dilemma. He wrote, 'If only I could thoroughly see how to defend the justice of our Deliverer in loving him the less by whom He is loved the more, and him the more by whom He is loved the less.'[5]

---

5   Augustine, *Homilies on the Gospel of John, Nicene and Post-Nicene Fathers*, vol. 7, Tractate CXXIV, chap. XXI, sec. 4 (Peabody, Massachusetts: Hendrickson, 1995), p. 449.

Modern commentators continue to feel the need to spiritually supersize this simple breakfast on the beach with the risen Lord. Nineteenth-century Scottish Baptist Bible expositor Alexander Maclaren saw this encounter with Jesus as a picture of the church receiving her eternal reward. He wrote:

> All the details, such as the solid shore in contrast with the changeful sea, the increasing morning in contrast with the toilsome night, the feast prepared, have been from of old consecrated to shadow forth the differences between earth and heaven. It would be blindness not to see here a prophecy of the glad hour when Christ shall welcome to their home, amid the brightness of unsetting day, the souls that have served him amidst the fluctuations and storms of life, and seen him in its darkness, and shall all their desires with the 'bread of heaven'.[6]

A Modest Message

Instead of lifting us up to heaven, this encounter with the risen Lord brings us down to earth. This is right where we belong. We do not have to look for hidden secret messages or layers of meaning in this episode. Food is the theme that links this simple breakfast with the conversation that followed. The risen Lord Jesus makes Himself known over breakfast. He supplies bread, builds a fire, and roasts fish before the disciples get to shore. In the ordinary course of daily life, the risen Lord Jesus makes Himself known. Basic activities such as working, eating and relating are the arena for holy communion, spiritual growth and vocational holiness.

---

6   Alexander Maclaren, *Expositions of Holy Scripture, vol. 11* (Grand Rapids: Zondervan, 1965), p. 356.

After they finished eating, Jesus must have said to Peter, 'Let's take a walk.' We surmise this from Peter's action when he turned and saw 'the disciple whom Jesus loved following them' (John 21:20). One wonders if Peter had anticipated this conversation, or did he dread it? Was he hoping that Jesus would ignore the past, or was he thinking of ways to ask for forgiveness? If you were Peter, what would have been running through your mind? It is safe to conclude that Peter knew that the conversation he was about to have with Jesus was important.

Jesus began the conversation on a formal note. By using Peter's family name, 'Simon, son of John,' Jesus returns to a time before Jesus had named him Peter, which means 'the rock' (Matt. 16:18). Jesus assumes nothing here. The question imposes nothing on Peter. 'Simon, son of John, do you love me more than these?' (John 21:15) More than what? More than the fishing business? More than this group of friends? 'Do you love me more than they love me?' Peter's own actions out on the water made the first two possibilities *non sequiturs*. He had, after all, jumped out of the boat and left his friends to haul in the fish! Peter understood the question according to the third possibility. He heard Jesus ask, 'Do you love me more than your fellow disciples do?'

Peter must have immediately recalled his proud boast, when he said, 'Though they all fall away because of you, I will never fall away' (Matt. 26:33). Back then, he had sounded so heroic. Jesus was asking him if he was prepared to make that statement now. His earlier actions, argues Leon Morris, 'showed that Peter had not wanted a cruci-fied Lord. But Jesus was crucified. How did Peter's devotion stand in the light of this? Was he ready to love Christ as He was, and not as Peter wished Him to be? That was the question, and it was an important one. Peter must face it and answer it.[7] George Beasley-Murray observes, 'Peter does not attempt to answer it in relation to his friends, but in his embarrassment he appeals to the Lord's knowledge that he truly loves Him, despite his failure.'[8] Peter answers emotionally, 'Yes, Lord; you know that I love you.'

Peter's response gives rise to three important observations:

First, his love for the Lord is no longer measured in comparison to others. He puts his old, immature comparisons behind him. His love is no longer competitive.

Second, his love for the Lord does not rely on his own self-confidence, but on the Lord's understanding of him. He is through trying to impress himself and others with how much he loves the Lord. It is not what he thinks of himself that matters. What is crucial is what the Lord thinks of his love.

Third, the Aramaic word the Lord used for love was translated into Greek as *agape*, and the word Peter used in response was translated *philia*. Of the two Greek words for love, *agape* has the deeper meaning. It refers to a love that is given by God, a love beyond our natural capacity to create. *Philia* is a more natural love that is evident in friendship and affection.

Does Peter's choice of *philia* instead of *agape* imply anything significant? Scholars have long debated this, but many scholars today hold that John used these two words for love as simple synonyms. We can safely conclude that Peter was not implying that he loved the Lord any less, but his choice of *philia* over *agape* may be indicative of his modesty. In denying the Lord three times, he failed

---

7   Leon Morris, *The Gospel According to John*, p. 871.

8   George R. Beasley-Murray, *John*, p. 405.

miserably. Did his denials cause him to hesitate about overstating his love? If that was the case, his reserve was commendable. Peter stands as a chastened disciple who knew that he had let the Lord down. His bravado is all gone. He now offers a more modest but no less sincere pledge of his love. He is no longer the flamboyant and egotistical disciple he once was. He has ceased to look down on others in order to build himself up. He no longer feels heroic in his own eyes. Instead of looking for praise from the Lord, he is relieved to be given responsibility. 'To his relief the Lord accepts his avowal, and indicates his reinstatement with the declaration, "Take care of my lambs"; Peter's love for his Lord is to be made manifest in his care for the Lord's flock.'[9]

Like a consummate psychologist, Jesus' three questions deal precisely with Peter's failure. Jesus 'does not frontally assault him with: "Simon, you said you were better than your colleagues! LOOK WHAT YOU DID! You said you would stick with me to prison and death! You thought you knew better than me, didn't you! You didn't deny me once, or twice, but THREE TIMES! And with cursing and swearing! Simon, What's Wrong With You?"' Such a rebuke, while it may be justified, sounds all too familiar. 'It is the voice of pagan leadership,' writes New Testament scholar David Gill, but 'not the voice of the Lord of hope and forgiveness.'[10]

Jesus' repeated questioning had the effect of searching Peter to the core of his being. It is interesting to note that when Jesus asked for the third time, 'Do you love me?' he used the word *philia*. Perhaps this is an indication

9   George R. Beasley-Murray, *John*, p. 405
10 David W. Gill, *Peter the Rock* (Downers Grove, Illinois: InterVarsity Press, 1986), p. 127

that Jesus recognized and respected Peter's more modest claim. By the third question, 'all the old self-confidence and assertiveness manifest in Peter before the crucifixion of Jesus had drained away. He could only appeal to the Lord's totality of knowledge, which included his knowledge of Peter's heart; he more than all people could tell that he was speaking the truth. He really did love him, and more than that he could not say. More than that was not necessary; the Lord accepted his protestation of love.'[11]

A Modest Proposal

Of all the things that Jesus might have called Peter to do, 'Feed my sheep' sounds the most mundane. Jesus didn't say, 'Lead an army,' or 'Launch a crusade,' or 'Compete with Rome.' Not even, 'Build my Kingdom.' There is nothing triumphant or glorious about this command; nothing complicated or sophisticated about it. Yet this little command, 'Feed my sheep,' led Peter into the large world of God's salvation. What Jesus did for Peter set the agenda for what Peter should do for others. In effect, Jesus says to Peter, *'Identify yourself with My interests in other people,'* not, *'Identify Me with your interests in other people.'*[12]

Peter was given no visions of heroic service, only the expectation of long-suffering, persevering, pastoral care. The sheep are in need of 'feeding,' not 'herding'; 'tending,' not 'catering.' Years later, Peter expounded on the meaning of being a shepherd in the Body of Christ:

> So I exhort the elders among you, as a fellow elder and a witness of the sufferings of Christ, as well as a partaker in the glory that is going to be revealed: shepherd the flock

11 George R. Beasley-Murray, *John*, p. 405.
12 Oswald Chambers, *My Utmost for His Highest*, reading for October 18, p. 292.

of God that is among you, exercising oversight, not under compulsion, but willingly, as God would have you; not for shameful gain, but eagerly; not domineering over those in your charge, but being examples to the flock. And when the chief Shepherd appears, you will receive the unfading crown of glory (1 Pet. 5:1-4).

The command 'Feed my sheep' is followed by a description of Peter's future. Apart from an authentic devotion to Christ, the description would be very unsettling and disturbing. Life was not going to get any easier for Peter, only harder. He was to find his joy and freedom in sacrificial service. His long life of service would end in martyrdom. He would embrace the principle of the cross, my life for yours, and encourage others to do the same. 'Beloved, do not be surprised at the fiery trial when it comes upon you to test you, as though something strange were happening to you. But rejoice insofar as you share Christ's sufferings, that you may also rejoice and be glad when his glory is revealed' (1 Pet. 4:12-13). Peter learned the truth of his own admonition, 'Cast[ing] all your anxieties on him, because he cares for you' (1 Pet. 5:7).

Peter's modest but earnest confession of love for the Lord leads to his simple yet sacrificial service for others. Peter was given the hopeful task of feeding and caring for his flock of followers. After warning Peter that he would meet with imprisonment and death, Jesus reaffirmed his original and permanent challenge: 'Follow me!' Jesus' first and last words to Peter remain the same, not only for Peter but for all those who follow the risen Lord Jesus. The invitational 'follow me' becomes the devotional 'follow me.' The initial 'follow me' becomes the everlasting 'follow me.' Do you love Jesus? Then feed His sheep.

Splendor in the Ordinary

Evidence for the risen Lord Jesus is not found in larger-than-life personalities or in high-energy worship services. It is not found in political campaigns or in morality crusades. People who attend Bible studies, sing in the choir, serve on mission boards and read the latest best-selling books on the successful Christian life are not necessarily our best evidence for the resurrection. Many of us are like Peter before the cross and the resurrection. We are eager, insecure, self-centered and focused on our own welfare. We follow Jesus in our own way, not His way; on our own terms, not His terms. We believe in living the good life more than we believe in living the resurrection life. We are eager, efficient and in control, but reluctant to pick up our cross and follow the risen Jesus into the daily routines of family and work. We need help to lay aside our insecurities and turn to Jesus. We need to know the freedom of Christ's love and forgiveness.

When seekers come to church, what kind of believers should they expect to find? The best they can find are chastened, humble believers like Peter, who, after an encounter with the risen Lord, are ready to follow Christ the Jesus way. They have heard the question: 'Do you love me?' and they have said, 'Yes, Lord, you know that I love you.' They love the Lord with all their heart, soul, strength, and mind, and their neighbor as themselves. They are husbands who love their wives as Christ loved the church, and wives who love their husbands the way they love the Lord; parents who love their children, not as an extension of their alter ego—not as immortality symbols, but as gifts from God; brothers and sisters in Christ who love one another, not because they belong to the same race or tribe or social strata or cultural background, but because they are one in Christ.

These are Beatitude-based believers, with salt and light impact, who practice Sermon-on-the-Mount obedience: love instead of hate, purity instead of lust, fidelity instead of infidelity, honesty instead of dishonesty, reconciliation instead of retaliation, and prayer instead of revenge. These believers practice the hidden righteousness of prayer and giving and self-discipline, not to be seen by others, but to be in communion with their heavenly Father.

These modest believers are known for practicing the rhythms of grace, daily worship and prayer, meditating on the Word of God and confessing their sins. They love their work—not necessarily their jobs, but God's mission worked out in daily life. They take back the drudgery and boredom of life by investing their lives in obedience and faithfulness. They are created in Christ Jesus to do good works, which God ordained for them to do. When they break bread with non-believers, their conversation and friendship point to the presence of the risen Lord Jesus.

These God-dependent believers know that suffering, not success, brings out the best evidence for the resurrection. Quiet faithfulness is their default position when the bottom drops out of their lives. Bedrock trust in God is their sure hope when their loss is overwhelming. Against all the confusion and heartache experienced in the world, they know the reality of *Amazing Grace*, not just the song, but the gift of God. They sing *Great is Thy Faithfulness* not in three stanzas, but over six or seven decades. These are the people who escape the cravings of a gluttonous, overindulged self by building friendships with people in need. They look after orphans and widows in their distress and keep themselves from being polluted by the world. They are the followers of the Lamb who go into all the world to share the gospel. They refuse to be conformed to the pattern of this world.

They live by the principle of the cross, 'my life for yours.' No one pays them much attention, but when you have been around them awhile, you begin to appreciate their depth. You know they are Christians by their love—by their *love*. This is what it means to look like our Redeemer.

> The risen Lord Jesus asked, 'Do you love me?'
> Peter answered, 'Lord, you know all things; you know that I love you.'
> Jesus said, 'Feed my sheep.'

Throughout salvation history, table fellowship has made it clear what kind of food the sheep need. Food for the mind to strengthen communion with God; food for the body to sustain physical strength; food for the soul to understand God's values; and food for the hungry to serve Christ and His Kingdom. Over breakfast on the beach, Jesus reminds us that He is impressed with a life of authentic love, true worship, and costly witness. He urges us to find splendor in the ordinary.

DISCUSSION:

1. Peter appears to be a more colorful, dynamic character before the resurrection of Jesus. What accounted for his charisma and confidence?

2. Why did Jesus choose to reveal Himself on the beach? What implications can we draw from this revelation for our own lives?

3. Can you describe an experience in which you felt Jesus confronted you the way he confronted Peter?

4. What is the relationship between service for Christ ('Feed my sheep') and devotion to Christ ('Do you love me?')?

Also Available...

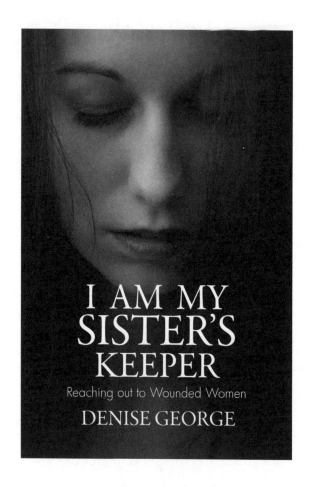

I AM MY SISTER'S KEEPER

Reaching out to Wounded Women

DENISE GEORGE

ISBN 978-1-84550-717-6

I Am My Sister's Keeper
Reaching Out to Wounded Women

DENISE GEORGE

And just as Jesus compassionately loved those who were suffering, so can we. *'As Christian women, our hearts ache with a world that suffers,'* author Denise George cries. *'Our love for God compels us to put our love into action.'*

I Am My Sister's Keeper tenderly addresses issues like broken relationships and divorce; unforgiveness; loneliness; spouse abuse; and loss and grief. Through biblical stories and contemporary stories of wounded women, George's advice guides readers in how to pray, offer a listening ear, share from their own experiences, and encourage others with God's promises. A complete Bible study guide makes this an ideal resource for groups of women to study together.

With the love of Jesus poured out through His followers, hurting women begin to overcome painful circumstances. Through our hearts and our hands, God still heals wounded women.

Denise George is an internationally popular writer and speaker best known for creative biblical application. Denise is married to Dr Timothy George, executive editor of *Christianity Today* and founding Dean of Beeson Divinity School in Birmingham, Alabama.

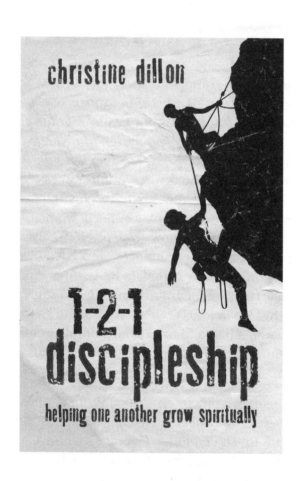

christine dillon

1-2-1
discipleship
helping one another grow spiritually

ISBN 978-1-84550-425-0

1-2-1 Discipleship

Helping One Another Grow Spiritually

CHRISTINE DILLON

Lack of depth and maturity in the worldwide church is a major problem. Very few Christians really know their Bibles well and can apply the Word to their daily lives. Few really live as 'salt and light' in a dark world. Most make little impact for the Kingdom or know how to share their faith simply and in such a way that people want to listen. Sadly, many are not even aware their Christian lives could be any different and so they live frustrated.

Could it be that we have failed to follow what Jesus commanded? His very last command before He returned to heaven was very simple 'Go and make disciples of all nations, baptizing them in the name of the Father, Son and Spirit and teaching them to observe all I've commanded you. And surely I am with you even to the end of the age' (Matt. 28:19-20).

This book aims to explain what discipleship is and give practical guidelines for discipling others. Christine Dillon says 'I feel compelled to write it because few seem to have been discipled themselves and good books on the topic seem surprisingly scarce. I was one of those who had to learn everything by trial and error. This book is the kind that I was looking for but didn't find. I hope this might ensure your way is a little easier.'

Christine Dillon is a missionary with OMF in Taiwan where she is involved in discipling and training churches. She says: 'Please also pray as you go that God will use you for His glory to disciple others.'

Diana Lynn Severance

Feminine
Threads

Women in the Tapestry of Christian History

ISBN 978-1-84550-640-7

Feminine Threads

Women in the Tapestry of Christian History

DIANA LYNN SEVERANCE

...a must-read for men and women alike, but especially so for young women who need to have a clear view of the contributions that women before them have made to the Christian faith.

Carolyn McCulley,
conference speaker & author

Well researched and well written, this study of "feminine threads" in Christian history makes for a tapestry of inspiration and instruction for all who love the Lord and his church – men and women alike.

Timothy George,
Dean of Beeson Divinity School, Samford University, Birmingham Alabama

Reading this book, we not only relish the voices and stories Severance brings to life; we also gain a hugely important understanding of an expansive heritage of women grounded in God's Word and serving God's redemptive purposes throughout human history.

Kathleen Nielson,
conference speak & author

From commoner to queen, the women in this book embraced the freedom and the power of the gospel in making their unique contributions to the unfolding of history. Wherever possible, the women here speak for themselves, from their letters, diaries, or published works. The true story of women in Christian history inspires, challenges, and demonstrates the grace of God producing much fruit throughout time.

Diana Severance is an historian with broad experience teaching in universities and seminaries.

Christian Focus Publications
publishes books for all ages

Our mission statement –

STAYING FAITHFUL

In dependence upon God we seek to impact the world through literature faithful to His infallible Word, the Bible. Our aim is to ensure that the Lord Jesus Christ is presented as the only hope to obtain forgiveness of sin, live a useful life and look forward to heaven with Him.

REACHING OUT

Christ's last command requires us to reach out to our world with His gospel. We seek to help fulfil that by publishing books that point people towards Jesus and help them develop a Christ-like maturity. We aim to equip all levels of readers for life, work, ministry and mission.

Books in our adult range are published in three imprints:

Christian Focus contains popular works including biographies, commentaries, basic doctrine and Christian living. Our children's books are also published in this imprint.

Mentor focuses on books written at a level suitable for Bible College and seminary students, pastors, and other serious readers. The imprint includes commentaries, doctrinal studies, examination of current issues and church history.

Christian Heritage contains classic writings from the past.

Christian Focus Publications Ltd,
Geanies House, Fearn, Ross-shire,
IV20 1TW, Scotland, United Kingdom.
www.christianfocus.com